MESSIANIC LIFE LESSONS
from
THE BOOK OF
RUTH

HOPE FULFILLED
IN THE REDEEMER'S GRACE

SAM NADLER

WORD OF MESSIAH MINISTRIES
CHARLOTTE, NC

"Messianic Life Lessons from the book of Ruth"
by Sam Nadler
Copyright © 2006 by Sam Nadler
Word of Messiah Ministries
All rights reserved.
Printed in the United States of America

ISBN-13: 978-0-9786568-0-5

TABLE OF CONTENTS

FOREWORD

I wrote this book because it holds profound and eternal lessons for all of us. The book of Ruth is a vivid illustration of the teachings in the book of Romans on salvation by grace, the necessity of faith, and God's eternal plan for Israel. All these truths are pictured in one Gentile who believed that the God of Israel would have her reach out to a lost sheep of the house of Israel. These lessons pertain to our personal walk with God, and teach us how this walk fits into the framework of the eternal work of Messiah as our Redeemer.

In this commentary there is enough direct application provided to make the revelation from the book of Ruth relevant for our lives. This book is written in a Messianic style, which is a Jewish cultural frame of reference, with the content expressing faith in Messiah Yeshua.* All Scripture is really about the Messiah and He is the key to understanding the Word of God (John 5:39). This fact must be assumed in the study of all Scripture.

Though no knowledge of Hebrew or Greek is needed to enjoy this book, I have added insights from the Hebrew and the Greek whenever the language helps us to more fully understand the meaning of the passage and how it relates to our lives. That Scripture should relate to our lives is the basic assumption behind this small volume. God's word is given in Scripture not only to inform us of what God is doing, but also to direct us in what God wants us to be doing.

In this regard, the Bible instructs us, "All Scripture is inspired of God and is profitable for teaching, reproof, correction and training in righteousness, that the man of God may be fully equipped, prepared for every good work" (2 Timothy 3:16-17).

There are many to thank for their assistance in getting this book into your hands: Carolyn LeMaster, Nancy Erkert and Joanne Cape for editing; Abby Mount-Burke and Natalie Ferrell for proofreading.

I especially want to thank my wife Miriam Nadler for her tireless work and faithfulness in editing and proofreading all the books and materials including this one.

I want also to thank Natalia Fomin, who oversaw the production of this book. Instrumentally, Natalia is a big part of why you are reading this book right now. I say "instrumentally" because when all is said and done, all those who have contributed their time, talent, and effort to the publication of this book would recognize themselves as mere servants of Yeshua, to whom each of us gives the thanksgiving, the honor, and the glory!

May His love, grace, and peace be with you all!

Sam Nadler

Yeshua is the Jewish way to say Jesus.

There is a glossary of Jewish and Messianic terminology on page 244 that may help you.

INTRODUCTION

The book of Ruth is traditionally read in the synagogues at *Shavuot* which means the Feast of Weeks, or Pentecost. The majority of the book takes place during the harvest period. On the surface it would appear to be a story about friendship, and that certainly is one theme. However, more profoundly it is the story of the people of Israel and the need for the Redeemer.

The setting of the book of Ruth: We learn that the story takes place during the period of the judges, "Now it came about in the days when the judges judged" (Ruth 1:1), that is, the 350 years prior to Saul becoming Israel's first king. The book of Ruth probably occurred toward the end of the period, during the latter portion of the book of Judges, as shown by the genealogy, which is only three generations before David. This takes place about 100-110 years before David reigned over Israel.

The time when the "judges judged" is also the time when two other accounts from the Bethlehem trilogy occurred: Micah and the Levite in Judges 17-18, and the Levite and his concubine in Judges 19-21. The Book of Ruth is the third work of the trilogy. Even though all three accounts concern Bethlehem-Ephraim, the first two accounts focus upon the flawed ancestors of Saul, whereas the third account is meant to focus upon the loyal ancestors of David. With these first two accounts putting Bethlehem in such a bad light, you can understand the delight of the women of Bethlehem upon seeing Boaz "achieve wealth in Ephrathah and become famous in Bethlehem" (Ruth 4:11).

When it was written: The earliest date that Ruth could have been written was when David was anointed King (1 Samuel 16). The latest that Ruth could possibly have been written was during the height of David's fame, as a later date would have probably required the inclusion of Solomon's name in the genealogy (Ruth 4:17-22). Therefore, the book was probably written during the early monarchy of Saul or David, but before the coronation of Solomon (around 1000 BCE).

The author of the book: It is traditionally understood and is accepted by the author of this devotional commentary that the last judge, Samuel, wrote the Book of Ruth for the following reasons:

- ✿ To provide a sketch of the pious ancestors of King David
- ✿ To emphasize the fulfillment of God's promises through Judah
- ✿ To show how the God of Israel provides for His people of faith
- ✿ To show how any dedicated believer, even a Moabite, is made part of His work and part of His people

Ruth's dedication to God became a picture to all believers of a life depending on grace and walking by faith.

The theme of the book: This pre-monarchial period is characterized as a time when people "did their own thing." The key text that provides a characteristic context to the period states, "In those days there was no king in Israel; everyone did what was right in his own eyes" (Judges 21:25, 17:6; 18:1; 19:1).

We find Ruth blessed mainly because she sought blessing in the God of Israel despite the lack of encouragement she received from her mother-in-law or from the culture in which she lived. Ruth insisted, "Your people shall be my people, and your God, my God" (Ruth 1:16). Therefore, we see the focus of the book in Ruth 2:12,

> "The LORD repay your work, and a full reward be given you by the LORD God of Israel, under whose wings you have come for refuge."

By faith, Ruth chose the God of Israel when others made their decisions based on what seemed right in their own sight.

The book is also about decision-making, both good and bad. God has no angelic cop to grab us by the neck and say: "Read your Bible!" "Go to congregation and serve Me!" God created us with the privilege of choice. With that privilege comes the responsibility of abiding by the results of our choices. Esau made a bad choice when he sold his birthright for a mess of pottage. Judas made a bad choice when he betrayed Yeshua for thirty pieces of silver. Ananias and Sapphira made a bad choice when they sold their land and then lied about it. Yeshua taught about a man who, in order to gain the whole world, was willing to lose his own soul. Now, that was a bad choice!

We will learn that making poor spiritual choices has serious and eternal consequences. Choices made according to the flesh may seem blessed at the time, but are often long-term disasters. On the other hand, choices made according to the will of God may seem daunting at the time, but they bring about long-term blessings.

Major divisions of the book:

The flow of the book of Ruth from Ruth's viewpoint:
    Chapter 1 - Ruth's faith
    Chapter 2 - Ruth's grace
    Chapter 3 - Ruth's courage
    Chapter 4 - Ruth's fulfillment

Although Ruth is the star, this book is also about Naomi. Through Ruth's godly love, we see Naomi's spiritual growth in the various choices – bad and good – that she makes in her life.

The flow of the book of Ruth from Naomi's viewpoint:
    Chapter 1 - Naomi's foolish bitterness
    Chapter 2 - Naomi's grace restoration
    Chapter 3 - Naomi's wise advice
    Chapter 4 - Naomi's full blessedness

Another key player in the story is Boaz. Though an older man, his life hints at the life of the One that the Jewish people need and will someday recognize, Yeshua. In biblical terms, he could be considered a "type" of the Messiah.

The flow of the book from Boaz' viewpoint:
    Chapter 1 - Boaz as the Hidden One
    Chapter 2 - Boaz as the Lord of the Harvest
    Chapter 3 - Boaz as the Kinsmen Redeemer
    Chapter 4 - Boaz as the Bridegroom

If you are like faithful Ruth, this book will encourage you to persevere in faith for a sure reward. If you are more like Naomi, this book can help you go from bitter, to better, to blessed. Let us all be like Boaz and seek to save that which is lost! Joyfully, the book of Ruth will reveal more of our great Redeemer, whom we can trust forever.

CHAPTER 1

NAOMI'S LIFE IN MOAB

THERE IS A WAY THAT SEEMS RIGHT TO A PERSON

Ruth 1:1-6 —Now it came about in the days when the judges governed, that there was a famine in the land. And a certain man of Bethlehem in Judah went to sojourn in the land of Moab with his wife and his two sons. 2 The name of the man was Elimelech, and the name of his wife, Naomi; and the names of his two sons were Mahlon and Chilion, Ephrathites of Bethlehem in Judah. Now they entered the land of Moab and remained there. 3 Then Elimelech, Naomi's husband, died; and she was left with her two sons. 4 They took for themselves Moabite women as wives; the name of the one was Orpah and the name of the other Ruth. And they lived there about ten years. 5 Then both Mahlon and Chilion also died, and the woman was bereft of her two children and her husband. 6 Then she arose with her daughters-in-law that she might return from the land of Moab, for she had heard in the land of Moab that the LORD had visited His people in giving them food.

Before Naomi Left For Moab

All people are influenced by their culture, and so was Naomi. Her culture is described in the last verse in the book of Judges 21:25, "In those days there was no king in Israel; everyone did what was right in his own eyes" (see also Judges 17:6; 18:1; 19:1).

Her times were those when "the judges governed." Judges decided private and public affairs and set national policy. However, they had no police force or standing army to enforce their decisions. Therefore, the context for Naomi's life is found in the times of chaos and anarchy. Proverbs 14:12 says, "There is a way that seems right to a man, but in the end it leads to death."

It has been said that the entire nation ran on the "honor system" for more than 300 years. In Judges 18 (which tells of the idol of Micah that led the Danites astray) and in Judges 19 (which recounts the murder of the concubine of Gibeah, which led to the virtual destruction of the tribe of Benjamin), we see the moral failure of the time when the judges judged. The anarchy came to be hated by the people of Israel, and led to the desire for a king who would end the chaos (1 Samuel 8). Samuel, a prophet and the last of the ruling judges, was sent by God to anoint the first king, Saul. When he was found unacceptable by God and Samuel was sent to anoint his replacement, Samuel almost made the wrong decision.

Samuel was sent by God to anoint the next king, this time from the family of Jesse of Bethlehem. When Samuel saw the tall, eldest son, he was impressed with his physical stature. However, as God instructed Samuel, we are not to judge by externals, but by godly standards.

God corrected Samuel for judging by what seemed right in his own sight rather than by God's perspective.[1] We often do the same, judging a book by its cover rather than by its contents. Contemporaneous with Samuel, the book of Ruth teaches what happens when we do not yield to God's authority and instead do what is right in our own sight. Naomi was certainly a child of her times.

NAOMI'S FALSE CONFIDENCE

Ruth 1:3-6 —And Elimelech, Naomi's husband, died; and she was left with her two sons. 4 They took for themselves Moabite women as wives; the name of the one was Orpah and the name of the other Ruth. And they lived there about ten years. 5 Then both Mahlon and Chilion also died, and the woman was bereft of her two children and her husband. 6 Then she arose with her daughters-in-law that she might return from the land of Moab, for she had heard in the land of Moab that the LORD had visited His people in giving them food.

What gives you confidence and a sense of security? A good job? Respect? Appreciation from your friends? Naomi had plenty of reasons to be confident: she was wealthy (Ruth 1:21), she came from the prestigious family of Ephrathites of Bethlehem in Judah (Genesis 48:7; Micah 5:2), and her husband was also the head of the family (Ruth 2:1, 3). When she lost her husband and her wealth, Naomi had a crisis of confidence.

---

[1] Samuel eventually anointed Jesse's youngest son, David, to replace Saul (1 Samuel 16).

LIFE AND DEATH FROM NAOMI'S POINT OF VIEW

"Elimelech... died." Why did he die? The Scripture is not clear; but the "and" that connects his death in Ruth 1:3 to his "living there" in Moab in verse 2 may hint at the cause. It is possible that his death was a judgment upon him for leaving Israel for Moab.

Naomi "was left." In Hebrew the word *sha'ar* found in this verse almost exclusively indicates surviving after a removal process, as with the "remnant" (*sha'ar*) of Jacob. As it says in Isaiah 10:21, "A remnant will return, the remnant of Jacob, to the mighty God." In this case, we can consider Naomi, an Israelite, as a type of Israel after the "time of Jacob's trouble" (Jeremiah 30:7), Jewish survivors after the tribulation. Like Israel at that future time, Naomi became a faithful remnant after she looked to her Redeemer (Romans 11:26-27).

Ruth 1:5 informs us that Naomi's two sons also died. The account of these sad events focuses on her point of view. In verses 3 and 5, Elimelech is identified as "Naomi's husband," not the sons' father. The significance of his death was her loss. There is no mention of how the sons felt at the loss of their father or how their wives felt at the loss of their husbands. The story now concentrates on Naomi. With the loss of first her husband and then her two sons, Naomi was devastated, destitute, and forced to beg. Understanding Naomi's sense of despair and destitution is essential to appreciating what will later transpire in this unfolding story of redemption and how God used Ruth as His vessel of grace. Naomi had probably felt quite secure in her husband's wealth and prestige, so it did not matter to her where they lived.

Now her husband and sons were gone and she needed to understand where to find her security for living. If we put anything in this life above God and look to those things for our security, God may have to remove them because they are competing for our trust and loyalty to Him. We need to see that the Lord is our true and eternal Helper, regardless of our circumstances. Isaiah wrote, "When Uzziah died I saw the Lord" (Isaiah 6:1). Isaiah realized that even after the loss of a good king like Uzziah who reigned for fifty two years, he had to look to the eternal and true King of Israel, the Lord.

Before we discuss why Naomi decided to leave Moab and return to Israel, first let us consider the decisions made by her family previously that caused her to leave Israel for Moab. Her husband, Elimelech, seems to have made decisions based on temporal circumstances, not on spiritual conviction (Ruth 1:1-2).

ELIMELECH'S DECISION-MAKING PROCESS

In Ruth 1:1 we are told that Elimelech left Bethlehem of Judah with his family. The famine at that time was quite possibly a chastening upon the land, but could it also have been a spiritual test to see who would decide to leave during difficult times? In that sense, Elimelech could have been escaping from chastening by leaving his trials and responsibilities.

He made the decision to leave the famine because it seemed the right thing to do in his own eyes. Some might respond, "But it was a famine! They were probably starving, desperate, forced to go to Moab!" No, not at all. Actually, according to Ruth 1:21 the text says that they were "full" when they left Bethlehem.

Rather than trust God, it appears Elimelech believed he would be able to keep his wealth by leaving Israel. We might pragmatically ask, "What is good stewardship in a famine? Is it not better to be safe than sorry?" I have one word to argue against that: Boaz. He remained in Bethlehem, Israel throughout all ten years of the famine, and he came out of it at least as well as he went into it (see Ruth 2:1). From Boaz's example we learn again that "Man does not live by bread alone but by every word that proceeds forth from the mouth of God" (Deuteronomy 8:3; Matthew 4:4).

Our obedience to God's Word is the best stewardship for our lives. God's promises are the place of safety; the safest place to be is within the will of God. For some it is also the hardest place to be, for it takes faith (Hebrews 11:1). Elimelech left the land of promise because his loyalty was to his own agenda and not to God's will. God's will is found in the promises recorded in His Word and never elsewhere (see Psalm 119:9, 11). He left to escape the famine; he made decisions based on circumstances and not faith. We should not judge too harshly, since we all fall victim to the same weakness, depending on how much pressure we are under and how bad the "famine" is that we are enduring at the time. Only Yeshua endured all tests without sin. This story of Elimelech and Naomi can be the story of any one of us when we leave the place of promise.

Elimelech went to Moab. In Ruth 1:1, we see that not only did Elimelech leave Judah, he also went to Moab. To his credit, Elimelech left Bethlehem in order "to sojourn in Moab." The word sojourn, *la'goor,* in Hebrew implies "to be there briefly," not to "dwell" in a land.

The root of the word *la'goor* means to live among people who are not blood relatives. Thus, rather than enjoying native civil rights, the *"ger"* (sojourner) was dependent on the hospitality that played an important role in the ancient Near East. Trying to escape your perceived problems is one thing; where you choose to go is another. In Amos 5:19, we read of a man who "fled from a lion and ran into a bear." That might fit Elimelech as well. He fled a famine and the end thereof was death. Moab was a place of death. Because of its earlier attempt to destroy Israel, Moab was a place cursed by God (Numbers 25:1, 17-18; 31:16; Deuteronomy 23:3-6).

Abram went to a land that God had shown him (Genesis 12:1); Elimelech went to a land that God had rejected. However, do not assume that a place that is rejected and cursed is drab, destitute, and unlivable. Quite the opposite. Because Moab had no famine, it probably looked good to Elimelech. Lot went to Sodom because it looked beautiful (Genesis 13:10-11). It was the character of Sodom that condemned it, not its appearance. Those who judge according to the flesh will always choose by appearances and externals. Messiah was rejected for this very reason. The prophet says of Him, "He has no stately form or majesty that we should look upon Him, nor appearance that we should be attracted to Him" (Isaiah 53:2). It was His character that revealed His deity, not His appearance. So despite appearances to the contrary, to sojourn in Moab was to go to a cursed place. It was seeking comfort from the enemy's fire; it was playing with sin for a season.

A trip to a place that God has prohibited usually has this false assumption: my trip into sin will be a short one, just a "sojourn," but as it turned out for Naomi and her family, it can mean many years of misery.

We may foolishly think, "I will be in the place that was cursed, but will maintain my identity apart from it. That is, I will be in Moab, but not of Moab." Those who seek sin, even for a season are identified as sinners, not saints on temporary leave.

Elimelech's short stay turned into a lifestyle. The text in Ruth 1:2 goes on to say that they "entered the fields of Moab and lived there." "They entered," in the Hebrew states literally that "they are there." When this same Hebrew phrase is used elsewhere, the idea is to be settled in, or there to stay (Deuteronomy 10:5; Joshua 4:9; 2 Samuel 4:3; 1 Chronicles 12:39). They integrated well into society and were at home. There were no feelings of remorse, no sense of guilt, and certainly no repentance noted. It started as a trip, but ended as a lifestyle. What started as a sojourn ended up as ten years of backsliding. No one starts out to be an addict, but the bad choices along the way – each small choice contrary to God's will – can lead there.

We read in Ruth 1:4 that after the death of their father his sons, "Mahlon and Chilion took Moabite wives." Their names have often seemed prophetic: *Mahlon* in Hebrew means tender, but also sickly, weak, diseased, or grieved (as used in Isaiah 53:3-4, 10). *Chilion* in Hebrew not only means completeness or perfection (Psalm 119:96), but also destruction, failing, and pining. We can all be like that: by faith, our weakness becomes an opportunity for God's grace to prove sufficient for us (2 Corinthians 12:9-10). Without faith, our weaknesses and failures can define our lives. The names of their Moabite wives may have some meaning as well. One was *Orpah*: in Hebrew this comes from the word for "neck." It has been noted that she would eventually "turn the neck" and leave.

The name of the other wife, *Ruth,* in Hebrew may refer to a female friend or companion (Exodus 11:2). Certainly she would prove to be a friend. However, taking Moabite wives was a sin in Israel (Deuteronomy 7:1-4; Malachi 2:11), like Solomon's sin in 1 Kings 11:1-2. The rabbinic paraphrase version of the Scriptures, the Targum, includes the rabbinical opinions within the text. We read in the Targum on Ruth 1:4-5:

> They transgressed the decree of the Word of the Lord and took unto themselves foreign wives, of the daughters of Moab, the name of the one was Orpah, and the name of the second was Ruth, the daughter of Eglon the king of Moab, and they dwelt there for a period of about ten years. And because they transgressed the decree of the Word of the Lord by intermarrying with strange peoples, their days were cut short, and the two of them, Mahlon and Chilion, also died, in an unclean land; and the woman was left bereft of her two sons and widowed of her husband.

Whether or not Ruth was a Moabite princess as Jewish tradition purports, we know that in Judaism marrying a pagan or any non-believer (let alone a Moabite!) was prohibited and that Naomi's sons were judged for this transgression. Some might ask, "Why is it so wrong?" Since marriage is a biblical invention (Genesis 2:24), what marriage means in the sight of God is important. Biblically, marriage is a covenant of joined values, not merely a mechanism for socially-acceptable sex.

Therefore, such a marriage-covenant between a believer and non-believer compromises biblical values and is considered spiritual harlotry before God, which is clearly prohibited. The New Covenant likewise prohibits believers from marrying non-believers for the same reasons (2 Corinthians 6:14-15).

Some might object, "But they weren't in Israel, were they?" No. And we are not in heaven yet either, but we still are to represent the God of heaven and the God of Israel wherever we live. We are His ambassadors and witnesses. Some might protest, "But what were their choices in Moab?" Unfortunately, if we put ourselves in a situation where all of our choices are bad, we can only make bad choices. By moving to Moab, their father had made this issue inevitable. When you move for business reasons and not in the best spiritual interests of your family, you can expect trouble. So Mahlon and Chilion decided by "what was right in their own eyes." That God later saved Ruth by grace in no way justified their sinful decisions. The end does not justify the means.

"They lived there about ten years." In truth, they did not have ten years to live; they had ten years to repent. We do not know how much time we have. We never know how soon it will be too late. That is why the Scriptures exhort us to "seek the Lord while He may be found" (Isaiah 55:6). God graciously removed Mahlon and Chilion from maybe an even worse evil if they had lived longer. As it states in Isaiah 57:1, "The righteous man perishes, and no man takes it to heart; and devout men are taken away, while no one understands. For the righteous man is taken away from evil."

NAOMI MAKES CHOICES FROM CIRCUMSTANCE, NOT CONVICTION

Ruth 1:6 —Then she arose with her daughters-in-law that she might return from the land of Moab, for she had heard in the land of Moab that the LORD had visited His people in giving them food.

We see here that there was a change in Naomi's circumstances. Her husband and sons were dead; she was left as a beggar in Moab. Naomi decided to return back to Israel. Why? Because she heard that "the Lord had provided for (literally, *pakad*, visited) His people." Perhaps she heard this news from the Jewish business people who traveled through Moab, since no Moabite would know God by His covenant name (*YHVH*) or recognize that the "Jews" were His people.

Perhaps Naomi figured, "I can beg better there than here," which gave her a more reasonable hope for food. Why would she think that? The Torah ordained concern and benevolence for the poor in Israel (Leviticus 23:22). The very Torah that revealed that she was a sinner also provided mercy to her in her desperation. The same principle applies today: the Torah shows we are all sinners, but also mercifully points to atonement in Messiah. God may have you in a famine emotionally, physically, or financially. Turn to Him, for He is the Bread of Life.

Even though Naomi decided to return to Israel, there was no change in her convictions. Naomi's faulty consideration for life remained: her return was based on a change of her circumstances rather than on her convictions. Prior to this time, she did not have a problem with Israel or Bethlehem per se, but returning to Israel had not been practical. Her desire to leave Moab and return to Israel was based on circumstances – she would return when it was worth her while. Many carnal and false believers will identify with the people of God and even with God if it serves their purposes. Naomi was no Zionist. She left the land for food, only to return for food. Like her husband and her sons previously, she was making decisions according to "what was right in her own eyes" and not according to God's Word. God's Word is our only guide for living and the very "portrait" of God so that we may know His graciousness, justice, love, and mercy more deeply. There is a way that seems right unto God, and the end thereof is life; conversely, "there is a way which seems right to a man, but its end is the way of death" (Proverbs 14:12). In this instance, though, God is graciously directing Naomi's steps toward His plan of redemption.[2]

The family left Israel, the place of promise, because of trials. They might have thought, "This is the Promised Land?" Yes, the Promised Land that could even have giants! The place of promise can become the place of testing. As we read regarding Abraham in Hebrews 11:9, "By faith he lived as an alien in the land of promise, as in a foreign land." And again in Romans 4:20, "yet, with respect to the promise of God, he did not waver in unbelief, but grew strong in faith, giving glory to God."

Trials of life, whether they come from physical, financial, or doctrinal issues will test you to see if you will trust in the promises of God or the world's passing pleasures. Do not forsake the promises of God; endure hardship as good soldiers of Messiah: bear up to chastening. As with Joseph, "Until the time that his word came to pass, the word of the LORD tested him" (Psalm 105:19).

Like a wise physician, God assures us: I may cause you grief, but I will not harm you. Do not evade the chastening of the Lord. It has a purpose.

---

2 "The mind of man plans his way, but the LORD directs his steps" (NASB, Proverbs 16:9).

An Emperor butterfly squeezes out of a tiny hole in the cocoon, squeezing the liquid in his body into his wings in order to expand them. A boy saw such a butterfly struggling and "helped it" by cutting a slit so it could easily emerge. But it was a strange looking thing that could not fly. It had been made to struggle before it could fly. We read this same truth throughout the word of God. In Isaiah 48:10 we read, "Behold, I have refined you, but not as silver; I have tested you in the furnace of affliction." It says in Galatians 6:9, "And let us not lose heart in doing good, for in due time we shall reap if we do not grow weary." Our struggles have an eternal purpose.

Can you imagine Mickey Mantle, the star of the New York Yankees, crying to his coach, Casey Stengel: "Every time I try to bat that guy throws me a really fast, curvy ball. Why is that guy trying to hinder me from making a home run?" Casey would have said to him, "But you're Mickey Mantle! You're so gifted, you can hit any ball that pitcher throws to you."

In the midst of our "famines" we need to run the race looking unto Yeshua, for in Messiah we are children of God. We are enabled in Yeshua to be more than conquerors (Romans 8:37). "While we look not at the things which are seen, but at the things which are not seen; for the things which are seen are temporal, but the things which are not seen are eternal" (2 Corinthians 4:18).

Chapter 2

YOUR GOD IS MY GOD

Ruth's Triumphant Faith

Ruth 1:7-18 — So she departed from the place where she was, her two daughters-in-law with her; and they went on the way to return to the land of Judah. 8 And Naomi said to her two daughters-in-law, "Go, return each of you to her mother's house. May the LORD deal kindly with you as you have dealt with the dead and with me. 9 May the LORD grant that you may find rest, each in the house of her husband." Then she kissed them, and they lifted up their voices and wept. 10 And they said to her, "No, but we will surely return with you to your people." 11 But Naomi said, "Return, my daughters. Why should you go with me? Have I yet sons in my womb, that they may be your husbands? 12 Return, my daughters! Go, for I am too old to have a husband. If I said I have hope, if I should even have a husband tonight and also bear sons, 13 would you therefore wait until they were grown? Would you therefore refrain from marrying? No, my daughters, for it is harder for me than for you, for the hand of the LORD has gone forth against me." 14 And they lifted up their voices and wept again; and Orpah kissed her mother-in-law, but Ruth clung to her. 15 Then Naomi said, "Behold, your sister-in-law has gone back to her people and her gods; return after your sister-in-law." 16 But Ruth said, "Do not urge me to leave you or turn back from following you; for where you go, I will go, and where you lodge, I will lodge. Your people shall be my people, and your God, my God. 17 Where you die, I will die, and there I will be buried. Thus may the LORD do to me, and worse, if anything but death parts you and me." 18 When Naomi saw that she was determined to go with her, she said no more to her.

Buying a used car? Test-drive it to make sure it runs well uphill, not just downhill! Real faith is tested faith and therefore triumphant faith. Some people's faith is tested by famine, others by dissuasions. In this section we read Naomi's arguments for keeping her daughters-in-law from following her to Israel. Traditional Judaism sees this as the pattern for Judaism's conversion process: only after attempting to seriously dissuade them, are you allowed to convert someone (Yevomot 47b).

Nonetheless, Naomi was not trying to represent Israel, the Bible, or God. After the many carnal choices that had left her begging in Moab, Naomi heard that God had provided food in Israel, and for that reason she wanted to go back to Judah. She might be characterized more as an opportunist than a Zionist, let alone an observant Jew.

She loved her daughters-in-law, but in her despair she saw no alternative, but to spare these Moabite women from further difficulty in Israel. As noted, bringing Moabites into Israel may not have been seen in a positive light considering the Torah's teaching on the matter (Deuteronomy 23:3-6). This may or may not have been an attempt to dissuade Ruth and Orpah in order to see if they were sincere in their desire to follow the God of Israel, but we can certainly see Ruth's shining faith contrasted with Naomi's dark despair.

Naomi's arguments were a testing of Ruth's faith. I have learned that everything we believe will be tested, so that which remains may be of eternal value. Thus Ruth's experience at this time like our experiences of tested faith reflect the truth in Hebrews 12:27,

> The removing of those things which can be shaken, as of created things, in order that those things which cannot be shaken may remain.

Ruth's faith was amazing: it came from the weakest of believers, possibly her husband, who had married a Moabite non-believer. How many people have heard the Good News because they married a weak believer? Though that never justifies a believer marrying a non-believer, it is still awesome to realize that some do come to faith this way. In light of the Scriptures (Deuteronomy 23:3-6), why did God accept Ruth the Moabite? Because we see that grace can overturn a curse, as with the eunuch in Acts 8, the illegitimate Jephthah in Judges 11:1, and us, as seen in Galatians 3:13-14. All manner of sin is forgiven in Messiah.

Naomi's arguments tested Ruth's faith. Faith that is untested is superficial and is not spiritually triumphant, because it does not depend on God; it relies on the flesh for personal fulfillment.

> Ruth 1:7 —So she departed from the place where she was, and her two daughters-in-law with her; and they went on the way to return to the land of Judah.

Naomi went out from the place where she was. The verb "went" is in the singular, indicating that it was Naomi's initiative and the others merely followed her lead. Since it was "to the land of Judah," the young women had never been there before. However, the text states, "and her two daughters-in-law with her," implying that there was no foot-dragging on the part of her daughters-in-law. Naomi felt responsible for them, and she realized that the women's intentions were not merely to see her leave Moab but to follow her to Israel, where Moabites were not welcomed. This made Naomi feel even more inadequate, for how could she ever care for them there?

They were on the way to return or more literally "on the road to return," *baderek lashoov* in the Hebrew. Naomi's "return" began like the prodigal son. In Luke 15:19, the prodigal son was willing to return in order to be his father's servant. Similarly, Naomi was seeking to beg where she knew she would be more accepted. Her "road to return" started in humility and eventually led to honor. Are you on the road to return? There is a way to come home. The road back begins by humbly recognizing your need to return. It starts by saying it would be better to serve the heavenly Father than to be away from Him.

The Counsel Of Naomi

Ruth 1:8-9 —And Naomi said to her two daughters-in-law, "Go return each of you to her mother's house. May the LORD deal kindly with you as you have dealt with the dead and with me. 9 May the LORD grant that you may find rest, each in the house of her husband." Then she kissed them, and they lifted up their voices and wept.

With sincere love for both, Naomi gave Ruth and Orpah her best counsel. However, a well-meaning but carnal person can only give well-meaning but carnal advice; a bitter well can only give bitter water.

Naomi's advice came out of her own faithlessness: since she was living by "what seemed right in her own eyes," she could provide no more faithful advice than she herself was following. You cannot give what you do not have.

NAOMI'S COUNSEL FROM NATURAL DESIRE

In this short section we see Naomi holding out the possibility of fruitfulness and a fulfilled life.

Her counsel provided some guidance about comfort: Naomi encouraged both women to return to their natural families: "Go return each of you to her mother's house." I am sure that it seemed quite reasonable to suggest that they return to their mothers: "Go where you will be readily accepted; get blessings where you can!" This was, after all, her original philosophy: "Go for the comfort zone, not the commitment zone. Israel will provide nothing but heartache for you; stay with your own people." But in fact, Israel alone had the Word of God (Romans 3:1-2).

Moab and their Moabite mothers could spiritually offer them nothing. Even positive counsel is bad when that advice differs from God's Word and His will.

Her counsel reflects a theory of fairness: "May the LORD deal kindly with you as you have dealt with the dead and with me." Like that of Job's counselors, Naomi's view of God is that He is fair: bad things happen to bad people, but good things happen to good people. Since you blessed my sons, who are now dead, and me you deserve a blessing. It is like saying, "I helped someone across the street, so God owes me a blessing." We tend to focus on what we did right, not what we did wrong. But according to the Scriptures "all have sinned and fall short of the glory of God" (Romans 3:23). God works by grace, not by fairness. For fairness brings eternal judgment, but forgiveness, not fairness will bring you to heaven and grace alone will secure eternity.

Her counsel taught dependence upon externals for internal contentment: Where is rest to be found? "May the LORD grant that you may find rest, each in the house of her husband." For Naomi, rest was found in the family. The word "rest" in the Hebrew *menoochah*, refers to a resting place, a settled secure home, and implies contentment of heart. Where is that rest found? Naomi was saying, "Find rest, each in the house of her husband." Can one find fulfillment and rest in a marriage where God is not the foundation? In Scripture, God is our rest, whether we are single or married. This is reiterated in Psalm 95:11; 116:7; Deuteronomy 12:9; 1 Kings 8:56; 1 Chronicles 22:9; Nehemiah 9:28; Isaiah 28:12; 32:18, and Revelation 14:11.

Once you are settled in the Lord, then marriage and a home can be the place to express that rest (as in Ruth 3:1). You have heard it said, "Don't marry anyone who has no *visible* means of support." Rather, we should say, "Don't marry anyone who has no *invisible* means of support." Until someone is resting in their relationship with the Lord, he or she will only be restless in every other relationship. Imagine our spouses expecting us to provide the rest that their souls need. That would surely be an unreasonable expectation.

The carnally-minded see their external circumstances as determining their internal condition: their marriage, house, car, kids, or career can determine the condition of their souls. So Naomi's initial counsel contained three steps to rest that included: 1) go to your mother's house, so you won't be a beggar in the streets; 2) expect fairness from God; 3) God's kindness is found when He opens doors for you in a new husband's house for rest. But we know that this advice is flawed, because it is the eternal Spirit of God that comforts the internal soul, regardless of the external circumstances. The eternal God alone can comfort you, for He is the God of all comfort (2 Corinthians 1:3-6). In the New Covenant, Paul testifies to finding contentment, regardless of his situation.

> Philippians 4:11-13 —Not that I speak from want, for I have learned to be content in whatever circumstances I am. I know how to get along with humble means, and I also know how to live in prosperity; in any and every circumstance I have learned the secret of being filled and going hungry, both of having abundance and suffering need. I can do all things through Messiah who strengthens me.

Yes, Yeshua is the eternal and spiritual secret we each need to learn, and grow into.

Yeshua the Messiah urges each of us to come to Him for the rest our soul desires and searches for, as it says in Matthew 11:28-29, "Come to Me, all who are weary and heavy-laden, and I will give you rest. Take My yoke upon you, and learn from Me, for I am gentle and humble in heart; and you shall find rest for your souls."

We can "cast all our cares upon Him because He cares for us" (1 Peter 5:7). In doing so, we are assured that "the peace of God that surpasses all understanding will guard our hearts and minds in Messiah Yeshua" (Philippians 4:7-18). Whose counsel will you follow, Naomi's or Yeshua's?

This short section ends with, "Then she kissed them, and they lifted up their voices and wept" (Ruth 1:9). They wept, and well they should; they knew what that meant. She kissed them meaning it as a goodbye kiss. You kiss when you meet someone you care for and again when you leave that person. When you meet, kiss, and then weep, it is from joy (Genesis 29:11, 33:4, 45:15, Luke 7:38), but when you depart, kiss, and weep, it is from deep sorrow (Genesis 50:1, Act 20:37). This was meant to be Naomi's final farewell (as in Ruth 1:14).

NAOMI'S COUNSEL OF PHYSICAL DEFEAT

Ruth 1:10 —And they said to her, "No, but we will surely return with you to your people."

Regardless of how effective Naomi may have thought her short speech had been, it seems that some people just cannot take the hint. These two Moabite women wanted to return to "her people" and not to their own people. You can imagine Naomi's mind at work, "That's just it, you can't return with me to my people, because they are my people and not your people."

Regardless of the difficulties that they might face in Judah, Orpah and Ruth had lost their husbands and had bonded with Naomi, and it was heart-breaking for them to think of losing any more family. To the pragmatic Naomi, this seemed sweet and sentimental, but totally unwise and impractical. As many readers may already know, real faith trusts God to provide His blessings so that we can fulfill His calling in our lives. But Naomi did not have much of this "real faith" and could not imagine these Moabite women being called to live in Israel. She had forgotten the calling of Israel to reach out to the nations (Genesis 12:3). Through several rhetorical questions, she provided further counsel to these apparently "sales-resistant" Moabites.

NAOMI'S REALITY OF FUTILITY

Naomi attempted to persuade them that accompanying her would be senseless, useless, and hopeless.

First, accompanying me is senseless: There is no significant purpose. Her plea was that they "Return!" It is in the imperative, and reflects the sincerity and frustration of Naomi's carnal mind. "Why would you go with me?" She asked, but it was her first rhetorical question. Her question implied that there was no practical reason to go back with her. "Why" has us consider the reason, and for Naomi there was no reason that would make sense. Her counsel of defeat would see their "faith" in joining her as crazy and purposeless, since it would not provide for their practical needs. The carnally-minded seek natural blessings; all else seems useless. The prophet Malachi observed carnal Israel in the fifth century BCE when they asked, "What profit is there to serving God?" (Malachi 3:14)

The first century New Covenant writer recognized the same trait in the hypocrites of his day: "The depraved suppose that godliness is a means of gain" (1 Timothy 6:5). There would be no service without some practical return. But since we are "complete in Messiah" (Colossians 2:10), all other blessings are overflow. We are encouraged to "seek first the kingdom of heaven" and all other blessings will be added to us (Matthew 6:24). To Naomi any natural blessings these two ladies may have expected from her were not available. Her cry was, "Please, don't bother knocking on a sealed door."

Secondly, accompanying me is useless: there is no reasonable provision. Naomi asked, "Have I yet sons in my womb, that they may be your husbands? Return, my daughters! Go, for I am too old to have a husband. If I said I have hope, if I should even have a husband tonight and also bear sons, would you therefore wait until they were grown? Would you therefore refrain from marrying?"

Naomi gave several practical reasons why it would be useless to accompany her. She insisted that Orpah and Ruth "Return! Go!" The reason for these imperatives is explained by the Hebrew word *kee*, meaning "because" and translated "for." They had to return to Moab, because she had an empty womb: "Have I yet sons in my womb, that they may be your husbands?" This second rhetorical question was meant to demonstrate the uselessness of accompanying her. She in fact was saying to them, "I have no sons to be husbands for you and that is what life is all about."

Earlier Naomi wanted them to find rest in the house of a husband because she only saw life as meaningful within a family and marriage.

Her next reasons are found in the statements, "Go, for I am too old to have a husband." Maybe she was implying, "The fact is, I'm too old to help you out." The Hebrew word *zakan* simply means "old." She reasoned, "If I said I have hope, if I should even have a husband tonight and also bear sons, would you therefore wait until they were grown? Would you therefore refrain from marrying?"

Naomi was past child-bearing years and even a miracle would prove useless. There was almost a sense of despair in this matter for her. What could she offer these young women? She felt like a useless old woman, so what could be gained by accompanying her?

Abraham and Sarah had proven her premise wrong by having a child at ninety and one hundred years of age respectively, showing that God was still the God of miracles. Life is fulfilled in service for God regardless of our age or situation. Some people live for God with a spouse and kids, and some people live for Him without a spouse or kids. It is not physical children, but spiritual children that we are called to provide (Matthew 28:19). We are never too old to have spiritual kids.

This seems to be what the Psalmist had in mind: "The righteous man will flourish like the palm tree; he will grow like a cedar in Lebanon. Planted in the house of the LORD, they will flourish in the courts of our God. They will still yield fruit in old age; they shall be full of sap and very green, to declare that the LORD is upright; He is my rock, and there is no unrighteousness in Him" (Psalm 92:12-15).

This is the New Covenant experience as well. As Paul said, "For if you were to have countless tutors in Messiah, yet you would not have many fathers, for in Messiah Yeshua I became your father through the Good News" (1 Corinthians 4:15).

For Naomi, these "disciples" of hers seemed like extra baggage, and she could not think of one reason for them to remain with her. Naomi meant well, but her counseling was discouraging and not edifying. It was given according to what was merely natural and not spiritual. In her fleshly mind she thought it was sage counsel. The New Covenant informs us that because of the truth of God's love in Messiah, all of our "words are to be edifying" (Ephesians 4:29).

Naomi's final argument speaks of her own spiritual dejection, "No, my daughters, for it is harder for me than for you, for the hand of the LORD has gone forth against me" (Ruth 1:13). In other words, she tried to say, "God's hand is against me! You need to hook your wagon to another star. I'm cursed. You can change location, but I'm cursed wherever I go."

Naomi was feeling spiritually hopeless. She knew a little bit about God. She knew that He is holy and that He judges sin, and she knew that God had chosen Israel and had rejected Moab. But what she did not know about God she filled in with what seemed reasonable to her in her dejection. Understanding that her move to Moab was contrary to God's will, she felt guilty. This guilt convinced her soul of the "separation from God" that sin produces (Isaiah 59:1-2). Indeed, the soul that sins is under His wrath (Romans 1:18). But of course, that is not all that is to be said on the matter.

What she did not know or reckon in her considerations was God's desire to forgive and not judge. For in the Scriptures God declares,

> Ezekiel 18:31-32 —"Cast away from you all your transgressions which you have committed and make yourselves a new heart and a new spirit! For why will you die, O house of Israel? For I have no pleasure in the death of anyone who dies," declares the Lord GOD. "Therefore, repent and live."

The New Covenant reiterates this same fact about God:

> 2 Peter 3:9 —The Lord is not slow about His promise, as some count slowness, but is patient toward you, not wishing for any to perish but for all to come to repentance.

Ultimately, the revelation of Messiah Yeshua is the greatest proof of God's love for sinners and of His eternal desire to reconcile them to Himself (Romans 3:21-26; 5:6-8).

Do you feel or think that "God's hand is against you" or that you are cursed, as did Naomi? It is true that God is against sin, but it is just as true that He loves sinners. Messiah was made a curse for us for He came to be our curse by taking our judgment upon Himself, a judgment that we fully deserved for our sins (Galatians 3:10-13). If God's hand seems against us, it is only out of love that He is trying to focus our attention on our need and on His desire for our repentance. That is, He wants us to turn away from sin, rebellion, and unbelief by trusting in Him and receiving His forgiveness for our sins.

Like Naomi, many are in need of good teaching in order to be "more than a conqueror" and "content in all circumstances" (Romans 8:37; Philippians 4:11). A man I met many years ago, Pat Johnson, was a drug addict and worse. When I shared Messiah's love, grace, and forgiveness with him, he was stunned and said, "I never knew He would forgive me." Sadly so many people today do not know of God's gracious forgiveness.

Because of all of the waywardness in my own life before coming to Yeshua, shortly after I was saved I still thought of myself unworthy of a godly woman for a helpmate. Eventually, I came to see in the Scriptures that by faith in Messiah I was fully forgiven, and a new creation. And God kept Miriam single just for me, and saved me just for her. Yes, the Scriptures helped me to understand just how much forgiveness and love God has for me and for all, who will believe in Messiah. But without the Bible's teaching on the full counsel of God (Acts 20:24), Naomi was left with nothing but her guilt and fleshly fear to haunt her.

NAOMI'S COUNSEL OF DESPAIR

At the very idea of leaving Naomi both women started weeping. "And they lifted up their voices and wept again; and Orpah kissed her mother-in-law, but Ruth clung to her" (Ruth 1:14). But in fact, Naomi's counsel had its desired effect upon one of the women, Orpah.

Naomi's advice, though painful, made sense to Orpah, who then kissed Naomi goodbye and left. Orpah's return to her Moabite people has put her in a bad light in traditional Jewish teaching. In traditional Judaism, this whole scene is understood as Naomi making sure that Orpah and Ruth were true converts before taking them to Israel.[3]

3 Targum on Ruth 1:16-17; Midrash Rabbah Ruth 2:16; 3:5

In the Talmud, the Rabbis saw Orpah as an ancestor to Goliath, and the difference between Orpah and Ruth played out in the lives of their descendants, David and the Philistine giant (Sotah 42b).

Of course, traditional Judaism is anachronistically reading back into the story these rabbinical ideas about conversion. Since Naomi was herself not living for God, it is quite strange to imagine her playing the role of Judaism's guardian against false converts. Rather, Naomi in her guilt and distress was in her own mind dissuading these women from accompanying her for their good as well as her own.

Ruth responded differently: "But Ruth clung to her." Was Ruth that needy and dependent upon Naomi? No, quite the opposite. All that Naomi was saying revealed Naomi's great need for Ruth. In response to all that she had heard, Ruth seemed to say, "So, Naomi, I see you have no one and nothing to offer, and you really need me to stay." The information that had dissuaded Orpah was interpreted differently by Ruth. In the New Covenant, Paul speaks similarly regarding his message about Messiah: the same message of grace is life to some and death to others. The same sun that hardens the clay, melts the wax. Faith in God interprets the same information differently.

Naomi was not quite done; she was determined to discourage Ruth from accompanying her as well. She said, "Behold, your sister-in-law has gone back to her people and her gods; return after your sister-in-law" (Ruth 1:15). This determination is once more seen in the imperative "Return (Go!) after your sister in law!"

This final word from Naomi was a counsel of despair that if followed, would have sent Ruth back to paganism. This awful advice emphasized three relationships that were meant to dislodge Ruth from her commitment.

First, Naomi mentioned, "your sister-in-law." This emphasized Orpah's and Ruth's natural intimacy based on shared experience. They were widows and fellow grievers. It is natural to seek fellowship with those who share similar experiences and pain. In such a group we can have natural comfort from those who know what we have gone through. This is all well and good, as long as it is a comfort that ministers the grace of God, and does not merely reinforce worldly values or encourage fleshly bitterness. We need to redeem our experiences from the depths of despair and not bolster negative attitudes about God, life, or others. True fellowship encourages fellowship with God. It is based not on some past grievous experiences, but on our future glorious hope.

We are to "forget what lies behind and press toward the mark of the high calling of God in Messiah Yeshua" (Philippians 4:13-14).

Secondly, Naomi mentioned, "her people." This emphasized the familiarity of ethnicity. In effect, she was saying, "You'll fit in better with your own people." But God calls us to identify with and reach out to all people in need.

Finally, Naomi mentioned, "her gods." Whenever "her gods" is used in Scripture it is used as a reference to paganism (Isaiah 21:9; Jeremiah 46:25). It may be hard for some of us to understand how Naomi could ever try to persuade Ruth to go back to "her gods" and paganism.

We may have never been so despairing, guilt ridden, and bitter (Ruth 1:20). In effect, Naomi was saying, "Listen, my God hasn't been much help to me lately. At least you know how to pray to Orpah's gods and how to seek them. Whatever works for you." I can imagine Naomi feeling, "I hardly know my own God, and yours can't treat you any worse than my God has treated me."

Naomi proves at least one point: you cannot commend a God in whom you have no confidence. The carnally-minded have so little confidence in God that they cannot commend Him. Those who faithfully witness for the Messiah are those who have confidence in Him. Those who do not share their faith are lacking confidence not in the ability to witness, but in the Lord they are charged to declare (Acts 1:8). In fact, you do not need "all the right words" to share Messiah with others, but confidence in His empowerment.

The first person to share with me was a new believer, who was probably the world's worst witness, but a seed was planted in my soul. I laughed at this person and mocked her for trying to tell me that I needed "Jesus Christ." I told her that I had so much of my own religion that I was not using, why would I want any of hers? About ten months later I wrote her a note thanking her for letting me laugh at her, for by then I loved Him, too.

Many people believe that as long as you are sincere in worshipping your god as you understand him, it's all that matters. But the Scriptures always condemn false worship no matter how sincere you might be. "You shall have no other god before me," God commanded at Mt. Sinai and still commands today (Exodus 20:3).

Believers are told to "flee idolatry" and to "guard yourselves from idols" (1 John 5:21; 1 Corinthians 10:14). We are never to seek for ourselves, nor counsel others to be involved in false religion, false worship, or false gods. Naomi may have meant well, but if followed, her counsel would fulfill the old saying: "The road to hell is paved with good intentions." There is One who is "the Way, the Truth, and the Life," and no one comes to the Father but by Him (John 14:6). Let our counsel and our lives always point people to God.

RUTH'S FAITH WAS TESTED

Ruth 1:16-17 –But Ruth said, "Do not urge me to leave you or turn back from following you; for where you go, I will go, and where you lodge, I will lodge. Your people shall be my people, and your God, my God. 17 "Where you die, I will die, and there I will be buried. Thus may the LORD do to me, and worse, if anything but death parts you and me."

Naomi said all that she could to dissuade Ruth and Orpah from accompanying her to Judah. Orpah left and went back to her home and to paganism (Ruth 1:14). But how would Ruth respond to this counsel of despair from Naomi? Would she take the not-too-subtle "hint" and realize that Naomi wanted nothing to do with her? Would she conclude that the best advice from the mother-in-law, whom she loved, was to leave? The way Ruth responded to Naomi gives us some valuable lessons about her faith.

First, we learn that faith withstands tests and perseveres: This characteristic of perseverance is especially clear in the original language. When Ruth said, "Do not urge me to leave you or turn back from following you," this might be translated as "Don't press me to leave you," or "Stop trying to force me to desert you or turn from you, and go after another." The word for "urge" is *pagah* in Hebrew and is used for doing harm, as in "fall upon" or even "kill" (Ruth 2:22; Judges 5:12; 1 Samuel 22:18). Ruth saw this as an attack upon herself. She had to withstand that attack and resist the temptation to leave.

Some might ask, "What would be wrong with leaving?" The word for "leave," *azav* in Hebrew, is used for deserting or forsaking as one forsakes the Lord in disobedience (Genesis 44:22; Deuteronomy 28:20; 29:24-25). In effect Ruth is saying, "I will not forsake you!" The next phrase, "turn back from following you" strengthens that idea of not forsaking. The Hebrew word *shoov* means to "turn back" and is used for "turning away from following the Lord" (Joshua 22:16, 17).

Ruth would not turn away (*shoov*) from Naomi because of Naomi's guilt and shame. Why? Because genuine faith in God reflects the character of God and that the Lord will never forsake His people (Deuteronomy 31:6, 8; Joshua 1:5; Ruth 2:20). As God reassures Israel in Isaiah 49:15, "Can a woman forget her nursing child, and not have compassion on the son of her womb? Surely they may forget, yet I will not forget you."

The same promise applies to us today as Messiah says, "I will never leave you nor forsake you" (Hebrew 13:5). God's faithfulness to Israel is abundantly apparent throughout the Bible. As Paul reiterates in Romans 11:1-2, "Has God forsaken His people? God forbid! God will not forsake a people He foreknew." And neither should we.

This faithfulness is reflected in all who walk by faith and have come under the wings of God Almighty, just like Ruth. As a Gentile believer, Ruth typifies the calling that God has for all the Gentile believers in regards to the Jewish people. "But by their transgressions salvation has come to the Gentiles to make Israel jealous" (Romans 11:11). Ruth was a sacred reminder that though Naomi had forsaken the Lord, the Lord had not forsaken Naomi. Ruth saw that the God of Israel had called her to minister to His people. Naomi, despite her spiritual condition, was still one of His people.

During Yeshua's earthly ministry He and His followers were committed to the lost sheep of the house of Israel, as is beautifully pictured in Ruth (Matthew 10:5). God has called all believers not to forsake His people, and faith in God is seen in faithfulness to His calling. This applies to every area of your life. For example, in your marriage God has called you to minister to your spouse, so be faithful. Faithfulness is demonstrated when you walk by faith and live to please the Lord (2 Corinthians 5:7, 9).

Secondly, faith calls us to associate with God's people: Why does Ruth keep using the pronouns "you" and "your" in verses 16-17? Because she is directly responding to Naomi's counsel in verse 15. Naomi implored Ruth to go back saying, "your sister-in-law, her people, and her gods." In turn Ruth responds point for point. Not "her" but "you," not "her people" but "your people," and not "her gods" but "your God." She had already identified with the people of God and the God of Israel. This identification is seen in four areas of commitment: personal, national, spiritual, and mortal.

Her personal commitment is expressed in verse 16a: "where you go I will go, and where you lodge I will lodge." For all intents and purposes Ruth was saying, "My life will be intertwined with yours, both where you go and where you lodge. Where you go, though you leave the land of my birth, Moab, and where you lodge or settle, even in the land of Israel." Ruth would rather follow a bitter believer like Naomi to the right destination, than to follow Orpah, a sweet non-believer, to the wrong destination.

Her national commitment is expressed in 16b: "your people shall be my people." God's blessing for the world is through the seed of Abraham, the Jewish people. "And in you [Abram] and your seed shall all the families of the earth be blessed" (Genesis 12:3). Identifying with God's blessing means identifying with Israel. Although the Gentile believers are part of the commonwealth of Israel (Ephesians 2:12), unfortunately there has been a cultural disconnect on the part of many believers in Messiah since the second century AD. By the seventh century, faith in Yeshua had lost all relevance to biblical Jewish culture and became unrecognizable to the "lost sheep of the House of Israel" (Matthew 10:5).

JEW AND GENTILE ONE IN THE OLIVE TREE

For some Gentile believers, it seems strange to identify with the Jewish people. In the first century, though, when the apostles lived, Gentile believers easily ministered within the Jewish communities. Paul uses the illustration of the Olive Tree in Romans 11:17-24 as a reminder for Gentile believers to show the kindness of the Lord as it was shown to them. The Olive Tree pictured the ministerial life of Israel and the priestly service; the roots are the promises made to the fathers.

These promises are to be ministered through Israel to the nations (Genesis 12:3, 22:18; Romans 15:8-12; Ephesians 2:11-22). Unbelief broke the natural branches off from this service. By faith in Messiah, Gentile believers are grafted into the Olive Tree along side Jewish believers in order to minister the very same mercy they received to the Jewish people (Romans 11:30-31).

Thus, all the first century believer's yearly calendar revolved around the feasts of Israel (1 Corinthians 16:8). They all understood and kept the Passover to honor Messiah Yeshua (1 Corinthians 5:7-8). They used the *Tenakh* as the basis for their faith and practice (1 Timothy 3:16; Romans 1:17), because the New Covenant had yet to be written (2 Peter 3:15-16). Like Ruth, let us not only love Jewish people, but also be willing to identify with them for God's sake.

Ruth's spiritual commitment is expressed in the phrase: "your God will be my God." Ruth implied, "I will identify with that which is unfamiliar but true, rather than that which is familiar, but untrue." When Ruth declared, "your God will be my God" it made no sense to Naomi, because in her heart she believed that God was the cause of her problems (Ruth 1:13).

Ruth's declaration is similar to Rahab's conversion and confession in Joshua 2:11, "for the LORD your God, He is God in heaven above and on earth beneath." Another example of a Gentile believer who had great faith in the one true God and identified with His people is the account of a Roman centurion found in Luke 7:2-9,

> And a centurion's slave, who was highly regarded by him, was sick and about to die. When he heard about Jesus, he sent some Jewish elders asking Him to come and save the

life of his slave. When they came to Jesus, they earnestly implored Him, saying, "He is worthy for You to grant this to him; for he loves our nation and it was he who built us our synagogue." Now Jesus started on His way with them; and when He was not far from the house, the centurion sent friends, saying to Him, "Lord, do not trouble Yourself further, for I am not worthy for You to come under my roof; for this reason I did not even consider myself worthy to come to You, but just say the word, and my servant will be healed. "For I also am a man placed under authority, with soldiers under me; and I say to this one, 'Go!' and he goes, and to another, 'Come!' and he comes, and to my slave, 'Do this!' and he does it." Now when Jesus heard this, He marveled at him, and turned and said to the crowd that was following Him, "I say to you, not even in Israel have I found such great faith."

Like the Roman centurion, Ruth the Moabite had remarkable faith in the God of Israel (Ruth 2:11-12).

Ruth's mortal commitment: "Where you die, I will die, and there I will be buried." This commitment was an addition to that made in Ruth 1:16 and went beyond anything Naomi was thinking. Ruth was willing to give up her Moabite life rather than be disloyal to Naomi. Did she have a fear of death? No. Faith can do that for you. Not that faith allows anyone to be cavalier about death, but the truth of eternal life overshadows the terrors of death. Therefore, all those of faith can say, "To live is Messiah, to die is gain" (Philippians 1:20). In Messiah "the fear of death is removed" (Hebrews 2:14), for He is "the resurrection and the life" (John 11:25). In the *Tenakh*, this same faith in the God of Israel, under whose wings Ruth rested, gave her the same confidence that all those of faith enjoy today (Romans 8:35-39).

The "Back to Jerusalem" movement among Chinese believers purposed to take the Good News of Messiah from China back to Jerusalem. The road from China to Jerusalem contains some of the most Gospel-resistant people in the world: Hindus, Buddhists, and Muslims. From the 100 million believers in China, many of whom have been forged in the furnace of persecution, as many as 100,000 will be needed for the "Back to Jerusalem" movement. This is a total life commitment. They are willing to die for this vision and are willing to say, "I am ready to die and be buried outside of China. I am a citizen of the place where the Good News is needed most." Ruth had a similar commitment. Moab was no longer her home. Like many believers today, she was homesick for a place she had never been.

Ruth then concludes her extraordinary response to Naomi's counsel with the most eternal commitment: "Thus may the LORD do to me, and worse, if anything but death parts you and me" (Ruth 1:17). This language was a vow, a blood oath. But notice the language Ruth used: "May the LORD do to me!" She vowed in the sacred and covenant name of the God of Israel. She confessed the LORD as her Lord.

Ruth submitted to the Lord and His covenant relationship. She was saying, "My life is in His hands for death or for life –I trust Him!" Ruth "believed that He is; and that He is the rewarder of those that diligently seek Him" (Hebrews 11:6). Do you? We enter into covenant relationship with God by the same faith as Ruth. If we confess Yeshua as Lord because we believe in Him in our hearts, we, too, will be saved (Romans 1:9).

RUTH'S DETERMINATION

Ruth 1:18 –When she [Naomi] saw that she [Ruth] was determined to go with her, she said no more to her.

Finally, when Naomi saw Ruth's determination, she stopped her dissuasions. Why? Because Ruth "was determined," and Naomi saw the futility of further arguments. The word "determine" is *ametz* in Hebrew and means resolute, courageous, and to strengthen. The same word is used in Deuteronomy 31:6, "Be strong and *courageous*, do not be afraid or tremble at them, for the LORD your God is the one who goes with you. He will not fail you or forsake you."

By faith in Messiah, this is what all believers receive. In Ephesians 3:16 we read, "According to the riches of His glory, to be *strengthened* with power through His Spirit in the inner man." God has given us everything we need to resist temptation and press toward the mark of the high calling of God in Messiah Yeshua (Philippians 3:14).

Although our faith is continually tested, it is a biblical norm and is spiritually good for us (Deuteronomy 8:16; James 1:2-4). We are to resist the temptation to forsake the Lord through obedience and trust in God's goodness and purposes, and we are to resist by the power of the Holy Spirit (Romans 8:4-16). Those who pass the "test" using faith are also faithfully rewarded (James 1:12; 1 Corinthians 3:11-15). God is revealed in the midst of the test. Testing produces testimony. An old illustration helps us to understand this better.

When a goldsmith refined gold ore, he would heat the gold until it melted and the dross would rise to the top. He would then skim away the dross and look into the gold. He would heat it some more, skim away the dross again and look into the gold. What was he looking for? He was looking to see his own face reflected in the gold. In the same way God is removing dross from our lives through testing, so that He might be revealed in us, even as we are being conformed to the image of the Son (Romans 8:29).

Is your faith being tested? Everything that you believe will be tested, so that what remains may be that of eternal value: "The removing of those things which can be shaken, as of created things, in order that those things which cannot be shaken may remain" (Hebrews 12:27). Ruth's faith was tested; Ruth triumphed by faith and the God of Israel was glorified in her.

CHAPTER 3

CALL ME BITTER!

THE RESENTFUL RESULTS OF REBELLION

Ruth 1:19-22 —So they both went until they came to Bethlehem. And when they had come to Bethlehem, all the city was stirred because of them, and the women said, "Is this Naomi?" She said to them, "Do not call me Naomi; call me Mara, for the Almighty has dealt very bitterly with me. I went out full, but the LORD has brought me back empty. Why do you call me Naomi, since the LORD has witnessed against me and the Almighty has afflicted me?" So Naomi returned, and with her Ruth the Moabitess, her daughter-in-law, who returned from the land of Moab. And they came to Bethlehem at the beginning of barley harvest.

Naomi's return was ignoble, but not unnoticed. In fact, the entire city was stirred by Naomi's return. Naomi left Bethlehem with a husband and two sons. She now returns without any of the men, but with a Moabite woman!

Today this could compared to an Israeli returning home with a Palestinian. The word "stirred" in Hebrew is *hoom*, which means in a tizzy, in confusion, or in an uproar. The Talmud comments on this passage in Baba Bathra 91a: R. Isaac wrote, "They said, 'Did you see what befell Naomi who left Palestine for a foreign country?'"

The women of Bethlehem wondered, "Is this Naomi?" The women were not asking her, "Are you Naomi?" They were asking each other: "What happened to her? She looks like a beggar!" Bitterness affects life and appearance. Because she was affluent when she left, her shabby return made an even bigger impact. It was like Bill Gates or Donald Trump returning in rags. Though Naomi's response hinted that the question taunted her, at this point one can only say that there was a tremendous impact when she returned to Bethlehem. Naomi's return was in bitterness and their rhetorical question gave Naomi opportunity to vent. She said to them, "Do not call me Naomi; call me Mara, for the Almighty has dealt very bitterly with me. I went out full, but the LORD has brought me back empty. Why do you call me Naomi, since the LORD has witnessed against me and the Almighty has afflicted me?" (Ruth 1: 20-21)

In Naomi's response to the women of Bethlehem, the first person form *I, me,* and *my* is used eight times in two verses. The simple lesson is this: A life oriented around self results in bitterness. Yes, Naomi did speak about God, but only to complain that He had ruined her life. From this bitter perspective, she could not bless the Lord. Naomi complained that first God hardened her; then He hindered her; and finally He harmed her.

Naomi's Resentment Toward God

Many names only have meaning in their original language. In other languages their meaning may be lost. In a story I read, this was brought out quite clearly: "On a cruise to Alaska, I saw my very first glacier in the magnificent Inside Passage. Excitedly, I asked the ship's officer what it was called. "It's some dumb glacier," he replied. Disappointed by his attitude, I bought a map to figure it out for myself. I calculated our location and found the name of the ice mass. It was called, just as he had said, 'Sumdum Glacier.'"

In English, when we hear the name Naomi we might think nothing of it, but in Hebrew, Naomi means pleasant, sweet, and delightful. The Scriptures teach that this "sweetness" is part of the nature of God, and it is referred to as His "beauty" and "favor" as in Psalm 27:4, "One thing I have asked from the LORD, that I shall seek: that I may dwell in the house of the LORD all the days of my life, to behold the *beauty* of the LORD, and to meditate in His temple." We also read in Psalm 90:17, "And let the *favor* of the Lord our God be upon us." Pleasantness, beauty, and delight come from relating rightly to the Lord. Apart from Him we find bitterness – regardless of our names.

When Naomi said, "Do not call me Naomi; call me Mara!" She responded as one whose life is characterized by bitterness. Her name was a cruel reminder of what she once was, but is no more.

In Hebrew, *mara* means bitter, fierce, or hardened. We learn about *mara* in Exodus 15:23, "They could not drink the waters of *Mara*, for they were bitter; therefore it was named *Mara*."

Naomi was admitting that she was a bitter well, angry, and hardened: "I've gone from Miss Sweetie, to Miss Sour." She gave an explanation as to why she was bitter, "*for* the Almighty has dealt very bitterly with me." The word, "for" is *kee* in Hebrew and means because. The Hebrew phrase, "dealt very bitterly" is a causative, or *hiphil,*[4] form of bitter. So she was saying, "I am caused to be bitter, hardened by God" (Ruth 1:20b). This is how Job felt: "As God lives, who has taken away my right, and the Almighty, who has embittered my soul" (Job 27:2). Maybe you have felt that way at times, or maybe you even feel that way now. You might think in your heart, "God did this to me! He took my husband, my job, and my health away." It is not uncommon to become embittered against God.

Naomi exemplified what is taught in Hebrews 12:15, "See to it that no one comes short of the grace of God; that no root of bitterness springing up causes trouble, and by it many are defiled." As noted, trials make you either better or bitter. Bitterness is a fruit of the flesh, a result of going through life's trials (*tsuras*) in unbelief and disobedience.

Naomi's miserable circumstances made her think she was a miserable person. Naomi identifies with and evaluates herself by her circumstances. People do this all the time. To see just how wrong this is, think of Messiah. He suffered as a criminal on the cross. We must be careful not to characterize and identify ourselves by our circumstances. We are not what our circumstances say we are; we are not what others say we are, and we are not even what we say we are to ourselves. We are who God says we are, and by faith in Messiah you are a child of God (1 John 4:2). Some might say, "But the Lord has shown me how weak I am."

---

[4] Hiphil: a grammatical term for the causative stem in the Hebrew language.

That may be, but it was not to make you bitter, but to encourage you to depend on His grace and thus become better. Whenever God chastens, it is for the purpose of our progress (Hebrews 12:6-11). Naomi's experience was like Job's, in that God brought her through trials in order to prove and improve her faith and testimony.

FROM FULL TO EMPTY

Naomi's resentment is shown in her statement that "God hindered me." Ruth 1:21a says, "I went out full, but the LORD has brought me back empty." Please note that she says, "I went out full" and does not mention her husband. The Hebrew emphasizes the word "I" (*ani*). In effect, she is saying, "I had it all: material wealth, position, prestige, respect, and two sons. I went out full." She left because of a food famine, but returned spiritually famished. God had removed everything she was depending on. He can do that. Luke 1:53 says, "He has filled the hungry with good things, and sent away the rich empty-handed." But often our trials are a result of our own disobedience and mistakes.

Morris went to his Rabbi for some needed advice. "Rabbi, tell me if it is proper for one man to profit from another man's mistakes."

"No, Morris, a man should not profit from another man's mistakes," answered the Rabbi.

"Are you sure, Rabbi?"

"Of course, I'm sure. In fact, I'm positive," exclaimed the Rabbi.

"OK, Rabbi, if you are so sure, how about returning the two hundred dollars that I gave you for marrying me to my wife!"

Like Morris, but much more seriously, Naomi's husband made a bad decision that affected his whole family. He chose to protect the family wealth in Moab by leaving the place of promise. In hindsight, Naomi might have realized, "We didn't know our blessings were tied to His promises, and that when we left His promises we left His blessings." Many of us may have done something similar and would like to have a "do-over" in our lives.

From Naomi's perspective, she came back empty. She measured her life by the externals rather than by the eternal. She evaluated her opportunities by her circumstances rather than by faith in the promises of a loving God. What she did not see was the blessing she had from God in Ruth. To Naomi, Ruth was no more then an extra mouth to feed. Naomi did not understand the value of a person of faith. Ruth, like Joseph in Potiphar's home, being a person of faith, became God's conduit of blessing. As Hebrews 11:6 reiterates, "Without faith it is impossible to please Him, for he who comes to God must believe that He is and that He is a rewarder of those who seek Him." Ruth was a seeker of God, and therefore she would be rewarded. Yes, as strange as it might sound, by faith Ruth was assured of a full blessing. "May the LORD reward your work, and your wages be full from the LORD, the God of Israel, under whose wings you have come to seek refuge" (Ruth 2:12).

DIVINE WITNESS AGAINST NAOMI

Naomi evaluated her life and concluded: "Why do you call me Naomi, since the LORD has witnessed against me, and the Almighty has afflicted me?" God judged me as disobedient and mistreated me.

The word "witnessed" in Hebrew is *anah*. It is used in several ways: to afflict (Exodus 22:23), to violate (Deuteronomy 22:24, 29), to testify against (2 Samuel 1:16), and to humble (Ezekiel 22:11). God's Word testifies against us in order to humble us. Humility is not only where God wants us to end up; it is also where He wants us to start out. Matthew 23:12 says, "And whoever exalts himself shall be humbled; and whoever humbles himself shall be exalted." Our humbling at God's hand is just to get us into the starting blocks on "the race that is set before us" (Hebrew 12:1). Before we can have the victory of the Promised Land, we must have the humility of the wilderness (Deuteronomy 8:3). He humbles us in the flesh to exalt us in the Spirit; He distresses us in the flesh to comfort us in the Spirit, and for us to become in His hands an instrument of comfort to all.

God's Word is His testimony of His own righteousness and His plumb line to see whether or not we are living as He created us to live. That is why God says, "You shall be holy as the Lord your God is holy" (Leviticus 19:2; 1 Peter 1:15). This standard has never changed. Yeshua says, "Be perfect as your heavenly Father is perfect" (Matthew 6:48). That is why Moses declared that if our people sinned, the Torah would be God's testimony against them (Deuteronomy 4:26; 8:19; 30:19; 31:28). As the Psalmist wrote, ""Hear, O My people, and I will speak; O Israel, I will testify against you; I am God, your God" (Psalm 50:7). The Prophets also warned, "Your sins have made a separation between you and your God" (Isaiah 59:2), and "The soul that sins shall die" (Ezekiel 18:4).

The New Covenant continues this theme as it declares, "The wrath of God is revealed from heaven against all ungodliness and unrighteousness of men" and "all have sinned and have fallen short of the glory of God" (Romans 1:18; 3:23). The sad fact is that "you are dead in your sins and trespasses" (Ephesians 2:1).

The Scripture shows humanity as we really are: sinners deserving His judgment, and therefore in desperate need of God's mercy, forgiveness, and salvation. However, it is vital to remember that if by His Word He testifies against us, it is not to make us feel badly about ourselves. It is to get us to deal with issues that He has always been aware of which we have overlooked, but need to take care of. He testifies against us not out of hate, but out of love, just as a doctor informs his patient regarding a disease that must be dealt with. Because "God is love" (1 John 4:16), everything He does flows from that love for us, even when it is to warn us to avoid danger. After all, if someone were unwittingly running toward a cliff, who would warn him: his enemy or his friend? God wants to make us His friends. As with Abraham, God wanted Naomi to be His friend and to walk with Him in fellowship. So also with us –when we heed His warning, repent (turn from the impending cliff of judgment), and trust in His mercy, we will find forgiveness and grace in Messiah. If we have been made His friends, then that same love should move us to warn others who are heading for that same cliff.

AFFLICTED BY THE ALMIGHTY

"The Lord has afflicted me" (Ruth 1:21). The word "afflicted" (*rah'ah* in Hebrew) means evil, mistreats, and caused me harm (Exodus 5:23). In saying this Naomi was implying, "I have become His enemy."

In this same regard, we read in Joshua 24:20, "If you forsake the LORD... then He will turn and do you harm." To understand this better, let us look at it from a different perspective, the perspective of the whole counsel of God.

Perhaps you have become His enemy because, "friendship with the world is enmity with God" (James 4:4). We are told, "Do not love the world or anything in the world. If anyone loves the world, the love of the Father is not in him" (1 John 2:15). By our rebellion, we may have become His enemy, but God is not our enemy. Messiah is the eternal testimony as to how God desires to treat His enemies. He wants to make them into friends. As Paul testifies in Romans 5:8-10,

> But God demonstrates His own love toward us, in that while we were yet sinners, Messiah died for us. Much more then, having now been justified by His blood, we shall be saved from the wrath of God through Him. For if while we were enemies we were reconciled to God through the death of His Son, much more, having been reconciled, we shall be saved by His life.

Carnal believers love the world and its things; they are friends to the system of this world and, perhaps without knowing it, are actively working against God. They are postured to see God's shaping, developing, and chastening them as punishment.

Unbelief has us at cross-purposes with God, and that unbelief can make us think that God is against us. On the other hand, faith sees that "God works all things together for good to those that love Him, and to those that called according to His purposes" (Romans 8:28).

A certain Bible teacher found herself seriously ill in the primitive outpost where the Lord had stationed her. To add to her sorrow, her check had not arrived, and she was forced day after day to do without the good food that she enjoyed, living on a miserable diet of oatmeal and canned milk. In spite of everything, she continued to improve, and after thirty days of a steady oatmeal diet, she finally got her check and was able to put something different on the table. During her illness she had "a little, sneaking suspicion" that the Lord was not "doing her right." When furlough time came, she told of her great trial to an eager audience. At the close of the meeting, a kindly doctor inquired as to the nature of her ailment. On hearing what the digestive malfunction was, he said, "Well, if your check had arrived, you would not be here talking to me today. The diet we always prescribe for that trouble is a thirty-day oatmeal diet." Despite what you may think, and regardless of the circumstances, God is on your side.

Looking back on this present world (*Olam HaZeh*) from the perspective of the world to come (*Olam HaBa*), we will see it all differently, for in heaven we will "know as we have been known" (1 Corinthians 13:12). We will be privileged from the upper side of the tapestry to see how all the loose threads and dark knots work together for His great purposes, which are to conform us to Yeshua and to be with Him forever.

This side of heaven is a process of spiritual development. In their comments on this section of Ruth, we see that the Rabbis understood this, for we read in Ruth Rabbah 3:7, "All His concern was with me, for in this world THE LORD HATH AFFLICTED ME," but of the Messianic future it is written, "I will rejoice over them to do them good" (Jeremiah 32:41). All afflictions, chastening, and corrections are by faith preparatory for what is to come. One thing is sure: God loves us and He is not our enemy – even if we are still His. Faith sees how all things work together for His good purposes, because we trust His character.

BACK IN TIME FOR THE HARVEST

Ruth 1:22 —So Naomi returned, and with her Ruth the Moabitess, her daughter-in-law, who returned from the land of Moab. And they came to Bethlehem at the beginning of barley harvest.

This first chapter of Ruth concludes with Naomi's perspective that not only is the work of God to be resented, but also the worship of God is irrelevant. We learned in Ruth 1:6 that the reason Naomi had returned was because "she had heard in the land of Moab that the LORD had visited His people in giving them food." This reasoning is reiterated in Ruth 1:22, "They came to Bethlehem at the beginning of barley harvest."

Like other seasonal workers, Naomi returned for a job. It was a good season for gleaners, who were barely a step above beggars. The beginning of the barley harvest was actually the beginning of the Passover festival, when Israel offered the first fruits of the barley harvest with the omer, or barley sheaf. We note this in Ruth Rabbah 4:2, "Wherever the words barley-harvest occur in Scripture, they refer to the harvest of the Omer." Thus the text states that she came back not because of Passover, but because it was the barley harvest.

Though the time of the beginning of barley season meant Passover, the festival was not the motivation for Naomi's move. She did not come back for spiritual reasons, but for more pragmatic aims: it was work time. I can understand where Naomi was coming from, because I once shared her perspective. While in the U.S. Army and stationed in Europe, a Catholic friend, Peter, and I (a Jewish man) went on a Protestant retreat not because of any spiritual interest in the retreat, but in order to get a free trip to Italy (where the retreat was being held). What may have been a spiritual opportunity to others was just an opportunity for Peter and me to fulfill our personal agendas. Naomi would have understood our motives completely.

Similar pragmatic motivation is seen in Acts 3 of the New Covenant, which tells of one born lame who begged at the Temple, especially at the Beautiful Gate. To him, it was simply a place to beg rather than a place to worship. His lameness (which contrasted with the Beautiful Gate) exploited the people's need to give a gift to the needy before they asked God for His favors. This attitude is not at all unusual. It is seen today in people who see the Christmas season and other "religious" observances as merely business opportunities. As is brought out in the third chapter of Acts, despite the lame man's personal motivation, God had other, much more redemptive, plans in mind for him.

Likewise, God was using Naomi's plans for His own redemptive purposes in light of His plan for her life and for even more lives than her own. This spiritual principle is seen in Genesis 50:20, where Joseph says to his wayward, but now repentant brothers, "What you meant for evil, God meant for good!"

God is working through all your circumstances so that His purposes for you in Messiah will be accomplished (Romans 8:28). Thus our faith is always in God and not even in the best of our plans. Take a moment and consider how your "opportunities" are reflecting God's redemptive purposes for you. Before continuing into the next chapter, take a few prayerful moments for a spiritual inventory.

Are you driven by your needs or by God's pleasure and spiritual concern for others? Do you have areas of resentment against God because of how His will has worked out in your life? Do you have areas of bitterness in your soul? Have you applied Messiah, the sweetener, to those areas?

In the next chapter we will learn that grace works. Naomi returned to Bethlehem with Ruth. Under the Torah, a Moabite had no place in Israel. How then could Ruth find acceptance there? She did not seek acceptance. She sought grace. If it was God's will for her to find acceptance and fellowship in Israel, it could only be by grace. The word, "favor" or grace is *hen* or *hain* in Hebrew and is found in Ruth 2:2, 10, 13. In the Scriptures, grace refers to God's unmerited favor. We see by Ruth's simple faith that when grace was sought, it supplied, secured, and finally, salvaged a lost sheep of the house of Israel.

CHAPTER 4

THE WORKS OF GRACE

THOSE OF FAITH SEEK GRACE

Ruth 2:1-7 — Now Naomi had a kinsman of her husband, a man of great wealth, of the family of Elimelech, whose name was Boaz. 2 And Ruth the Moabitess said to Naomi, "Please let me go to the field and glean among the ears of grain after one in whose sight I may find favor." And she said to her, "Go, my daughter." 3 So she departed and went and gleaned in the field after the reapers; and she happened to come to the portion of the field belonging to Boaz, who was of the family of Elimelech. 4 Now behold, Boaz came from Bethlehem and said to the reapers, "May the LORD be with you." And they said to him, "May the LORD bless you." 5 Then Boaz said to his servant who was in charge of the reapers, "Whose young woman is this?" 6 The servant in charge of the reapers replied, "She is the young Moabite woman who returned with Naomi from the land of Moab. 7 And she said, 'Please let me glean and gather after the reapers among the sheaves.' Thus she came and has remained from the morning until now; she has been sitting in the house for a little while."

In this section, Ruth seeks grace. Her confidence in God moved her to take steps of faith as she trusted the Lord for His provision for her life. In Ruth 2:1, we are introduced to Boaz, who will be a main character and protagonist in this book. This verse is parenthetical and is meant to set up the remainder of chapter two and the book as a whole. We know that God is orchestrating these events around His will as He does throughout the Scriptures and history.

BOAZ INTRODUCED

> Ruth 2:1 –Now Naomi had a relative of her husband, a man of great wealth, of the family of Elimelech, whose name was Boaz.

First, Boaz was a "relative," also translated as "a kinsman" in some versions. Ruth 2:20 is the first of twenty-two instances where the Hebrew word, *goel* (kinsman-redeemer) is used, but it is not used in this verse. The word used here implies that he is the one who knows Naomi's life. The word "relative" in Ruth 2:1 is the Hebrew word *modah*, that is, from the root word "to know" and implies that the kinsman is one who knows you well. In Proverbs 7:4, this word has the idea of an "intimate friend" as well as a relative. In English we might say that Boaz is an intimate of the family and "familiar" with those involved in their issues.

In this regard we can see that for Naomi, despite her moral failures, Boaz will show himself to be a "friend that is closer than a brother" (Proverbs 18:24), even as our Messiah was also a called a "friend of sinners" (Matthew 11:19). Yes, Yeshua intimately knows His sheep (John 10:25-27).

Secondly, Boaz was "a man of great wealth," that is, one who can actually help. The Hebrew that describes this man, *chayil gibbor,* is literally "[a man of] powerful might." In its various uses in the Hebrew Scriptures it can mean a mighty man of power, a valiant warrior, mighty of valor, and the brave warrior (Judges 11:1; 1 Samuel 9:1; 1 Kings 11:28; 2 Kings 5:1).

Since the world understands that "money is power" and since Boaz is a landowner of substance, his power may well have been equated with his wealth (Ruth 2:4-9). As we might say, he had clout, or influence in the community.

With this idea of influence in mind, we can understand why in Baba Bathra 91a, rabbis identify Boaz with the judge Ibzan (Judges 12:8-10). Though there is no historical or biblical evidence to connect these two biblical figures, we can appreciate the reasoning because of the clout of Boaz. We can more easily connect Boaz as a type of the true Judge with infinite clout —the Messiah. This idea of *gibbor* is used for the Messiah, who is called *El Gibbor,* the Mighty God, in Isaiah 9:6 and 10:21. Messiah enables us to be all that we are created and called to be. When we have Him on our side, we will never be powerless again.

Thirdly, Boaz was family; that is, one who would have a sense of responsibility for Naomi. Literally, Boaz was *mishpachah*[5] as we say in Yiddish or Hebrew.

Though translated "family," the Hebrew *mishpachah* is understood as a family in a broader sense than we generally use in English and would be closer to a clan relationship.

---

[5] Mishpachah: the entire family network of relatives by blood or marriage (and sometimes close friends).

It most often refers to a tight circle of blood relatives with strong ties, as opposed to people just living in the same house. This distinction is seen in Joshua 7:14. *Mishpachah* or "family" carries a sense of responsibility and loyalty, as in Judges 18:2 and 18:11, where it is assumed that those of the same *mishpachah* will protect and look out for each other.

One stereotype about Jews is that we are "clannish," in that we tend to stick together. This may have been necessary during the times in our history when we could only trust fellow Jews, but it has developed into a tradition of benevolence by the Jewish community towards the larger community around them. However, the idea of clannishness helps us to understand the sense of *mishpachah*. It also helps us understand why later on in Chapter 2 of Ruth, Boaz goes out of his way to assist and protect both Ruth and Naomi.

With such a family connection, we might wonder why Naomi did not ask Boaz directly for help. As will be developed more fully later on, under Mosaic Law (*Torah*), the brother of the dead man (*levir*), was to raise up a seed with the widow[6]. Boaz was a potential *levir*, but he was not the closest relative who was responsible to maintain the family line. To fulfill the duty of *levir*, he would have had to be approached for the responsibility. As Ruth 3 and 4 will show, it was Naomi's place to ask Boaz to assist in this way. Her reticence might have come from her sense of shame: she had left Israel with her husband because of the famine, while Boaz stayed and was blessed by the Lord.

---

[6] In other words, the *levir* was to marry the widow and have children that would be credited to the dead husband.

Perhaps she felt that she could not beg from relatives, but would bear her own burdens and glean grain. "Plus," she might have conjectured, "how do I explain this Moabite girl?" From what she says in Ruth 1:20-21, Naomi seems to have been resigned to her fate, as a hopeless, almost pitiful person.

Regardless of Naomi's lack of initiative in approaching her close relative, Boaz in this matter reminds us of our Messiah. Through the incarnation, Yeshua shares in our flesh and blood. He is always with us to protect us. The Scripture speaks of Him in this regard in Hebrews 2:14, "Therefore, since the children share in flesh and blood, He Himself likewise also partook of the same." As our "blood relative," he shed His blood that we might live despite the work of the enemy. Even now, Messiah waits for us to approach in faith and will then provide atonement and new life for any who believe.

In Ruth 2:1, even Boaz's name is suggestive of his role in this record of events. His name was used for one of the pillars in Solomon's Temple (1 Kings 7:21), and in that context was understood by the rabbis as "in strength." This is seen by how they translated Boaz into the Greek, *isxus,* in the Septuagint. The Hebrew of Boaz would be understood as "*Beh*" for "in" and "*oze*" for strength or might, as in Micah 5:4. It is a fitting name for a pillar and a fitting name for Boaz as well. Though most of us rarely live up to our names, Boaz certainly became a strong pillar for Naomi and Ruth. Even here, he is a beautiful picture of Messiah, of whom it is said in Revelation 5:12, "Worthy is the Lamb, who was slain, to receive ... strength (*isxus*)." As this strong Boaz made a critical difference to these women, so Messiah can make an even greater difference to all who trust in Him, as is promised in Ephesians 1:19, "The surpassing greatness of His power toward us who believe, in accordance with the working of the strength of His might (*isxus*)." Not only can all believers overcome because of Messiah's might (Romans 8:28), but we also have the hope-filled promise of Revelation 3:12, "He who overcomes, I will make him a pillar in the temple of My God." Like Boaz, in Messiah we can be a pillar by God's power.

THOSE SEEKING GRACE STEP OUT IN FAITH

Ruth 2:2 —And Ruth the Moabitess said to Naomi, "Please let me go to the field and glean among the ears of grain after one in whose sight I may find favor." And she said to her, "Go, my daughter."

In Ruth 2:2 we also see the principle of faith-seeking-grace, as faith knows that grace must be sought even in the most practical issues of life. First we see Ruth's willingness to work in her request to "let me glean grain." The Gezer Calendar sets forth the harvest seasons in ancient Israel. Olives were harvested from the middle of September to the middle of November. Trees were beaten with long sticks (Deuteronomy 24:20; Isaiah 17:6). Flax was harvested in March-April by cutting it off at the ground, then allowing the stalks to be softened (called retting) by dew or other moisture (Joshua 2:6). In April or early May, the barley harvest took place, with the wheat harvest in May-June. The harvesting of figs, grapes, pomegranates, and summer fruits was during August and September. Since it was already barley harvest time, it was too late to plant on Naomi's land, so it was glean or starve. This idea of gleaning is used twelve times in chapter 2 of Ruth and is a major theme of this section.

Gleaning grain meant bending and picking up loose grains that were accidentally overlooked by the reapers or were too few to matter (as pictured in Isaiah 17:5-6). In Psalm 104:28, this word is used to picture how a grazing animal gathered its food. This was also how the manna was collected in Exodus 16, as people bent over to pick it up off the ground. It was a humble way to acquire something to eat and at times may have seemed like taking other people's leftovers from their trash.

In *Torah*, Israel is warned not to reap the corners of their fields or gather the gleanings of the harvest; the gleanings were to be left for "the poor and the resident alien" (Leviticus 19:9-10, 23:22; Deuteronomy 24:19-22). Ruth fit both categories. Deuteronomy 24:19-22 gives a bit more insight into gleaning. The unharvested sheaf of grain was to be left for the needy, so that the Lord's blessing would rest on the owner's work (Deuteronomy 24:19). In the olive harvest, the trees were only to be beaten once with rods to gather the olives (Deuteronomy 24:20). The olives that were left behind were for the widow, the orphan, and the alien. During the grape harvest, the vines were gone over only once so that the needy could have the remainder (Deuteronomy 24:21). This generosity allowed the needy to collect all that was not initially harvested.

This was the compassion that God's law required; a benevolence that allowed the poor and alien to work by gleaning. There were no free handouts for healthy and able-bodied people. The benevolence was that they were given some work so that they might eat, although often just barely.

A miserable day's work of gleaning under the hot Middle East sun netted only the little grain that the reapers could not easily reach. But as noted, it was either glean or starve. Grace never encourages laziness; the faithful who seek and depend on grace are hard workers. Paul uses this same principle in 1 Timothy 5:3-16 regarding widows, who were to serve their congregation.

Underlying these benevolent rules was a concern for the needy. Israel was told to consider the poor so that they would remember that they had been redeemed from Egypt (Deuteronomy 24:22). Just as it is easier to steer a ship if it is moving, so God can do more for the diligent than for the lazy. He does not reinforce laziness with His blessing.

Just as our English word "please" means to ask respectfully for permission, so Ruth used the Hebrew word *nah*, which is translated "under," to ask Naomi for permission to go and glean. Though Naomi was not spiritually-minded like Ruth, just desperate for food, she gave her consent to Ruth's request. Ruth knew that her younger age gave her more strength than the older woman to glean, and she also recognized Naomi's authority as her mother-in-law.

This is commonly seen in godly homes, where the head of the house is allowed to initiate prayer at the meal. Faith takes the initiative to love and to live, but it shows respect for the elders God has placed in one's life. Ruth's willingness and humility of faith was seen in her asking permission to glean grain. No bitterness, no poor attitude —such faith shines through in the humble spirit that was pleased to serve as the Lord gave opportunity.

Second, in Ruth 2:2 we see her wisdom of faith, for she wanted to go "after him in whose eyes I find grace." This expression is always used by a person of inferior status in reference to a superior (Genesis 32:5; Exodus 33:13). To "find grace" means that as God opened a door for work, she would walk through it. Why did Ruth feel a need to find favor regarding work? Her desire to find a field where she would be favorably received reflected her knowledge of how the poor foreigner was treated by hostile landowners. It may also have shown her awareness of being a foreigner. Out of the twelve occurrences of the name Ruth, "the Moabitess" is added five times as a reminder that she was an alien and especially needed grace. The potential danger for Ruth was understood and emphasized throughout this chapter: "not to touch you" (2:9); "do not humble her" in 2:15; do not "rebuke her" (2:16); and "lest others fall on you (harm you)" (2:22). Ruth was poor, virtually a beggar, without any resources to insulate her from insults and rebukes. She was a single woman, a widow with no one to protect her. She was a Moabite, not merely a foreigner, but one from a despised land, and so she was without the respect of a citizen.

Third, we see her opportunity of faith. One may well ask if it was something she should have done at all if it was dangerous. What choice did she have? There is a difference between something dangerous, but not morally wrong, and something dangerous and morally wrong. It is never God's will to do what is morally wrong, even if it is safe. However, God does not forbid us from doing what is difficult as long as we do it depending on Him (Acts 20:22-24).

For that matter, it is wrong to do what is even very easy without trusting the Lord. Going to the Middle East may be death-defying, but it is not necessarily morally wrong as long as one trusts in the Lord for His power and lives for His purposes.

His grace is sufficient, and the safest place to be is in His will. Why didn't Naomi join Ruth in the gleaning of grain? It may have been her age, or it may have been the potential dangers that necessitated a faith that Naomi may have lacked at that time. Why did Naomi permit Ruth to glean if it was dangerous? It was either glean or starve. There are not always other choices. It reminds me of the flight on El Al airline to Israel. When the flight attendant asked,

"Would you like dinner?"

I asked, "What are my choices?"

"Yes or no," she replied.

Many feel like they have no choices in their jobs or relationships. But in the midst of our difficult circumstances, we do have a choice: we can and should seek grace in our time of need. But remember, we need to "find" this grace. The Hebrew word, *matza,* or "find," as in "to find grace," implies the need to seek. Generally, we only find when we seek. Moses wrote in Deuteronomy 4:29, "If you seek the Lord, you shall find Him." Yeshua likewise assured us, "Seek and you shall find" (Matthew 7:7). In fact, we are exhorted by the Scriptures not to waste time, but to seek His grace while we can: "Seek the Lord, while He may be found" (Isaiah 55:6). There comes a time, as in the days of Noah, that doors of opportunity are closed (Genesis 7:16).

You never know how soon it will be too late. But when we seek His grace, then we find His grace to be sufficient. Ruth needed grace in order to live as the God of Israel would have her live, faithfully.

PROVIDENTIALLY LED IN FAITH

Ruth 2:3 —So she departed and went and gleaned in the field after the reapers; and she happened to come to the portion of the field belonging to Boaz, who was of the family of Elimelech.

In this verse we see that the very grace that we seek guides us, because God oversees His world. God can be trusted through the ordinary and distressing problems of life. We see God's providence at work. The text simply states "she happened to come," literally means, "it happened as it was happening." When Ruth happens to choose one field among the many possible fields to glean, it alludes to the sovereignty of God over events in the lives of individuals.

This is a basic assumption of the Jewish faith and Jewish existence. We read in Exodus 23:20,

Behold, I am going to send an angel before you to guard you along the way, and to bring you into the place which I have prepared.

The book of Ruth revolves around this fact of God's providence. From the perspective of Ruth and Boaz, the meeting was accidental, but not from Naomi's perspective, nor from God's (Ruth 2:20). The Bible assumes God's oversight of our lives through providence.

We read in Psalm 37:23, "The steps of a man are established by the LORD." His overseeing providence in our lives provides these assurances:

1 Samuel 2:9 —He keeps the feet of His godly ones.

Proverbs 16:9 —The mind of man plans his way, but the LORD directs his steps.

1 Thessalonians 5:24 —Faithful is He who calls you, and He also will bring it to pass.

Because He oversees our lives, by faith we can be confident in Him. Even the truth of Messiah's coming depended on this fact, since He was to be born of the ancestors of Ruth and Boaz (Matthew 1:5). Indeed, we see this as God's providence through faith as Ruth moves ahead to look for work and find grace. The English translation says at the beginning of the verse, "And she came," which is a form of the Hebrew word, *bo,* which means to come or enter and is used significantly throughout this chapter in Ruth 2:3, 4, 7, 12, and 18. Ruth had first *"come* under His wings" in Ruth 2:12, so everywhere she went, she went by that same grace, which reflected her faith as she moved forward in God's will. Likewise, when we come to the Lord in faith, we will follow Him in all that we do, because the grace that we find in His presence providentially leads us.

Many in Scripture are providentially led, like the Magi in Matthew 2:2, and Paul in Acts 16. All are examples of God giving guidance by grace. We see this in history as well. Alexander Mackay prepared for work in Madagascar, but he was directed to Uganda to aid in founding one of the most remarkable missions in the world.

William Carey proposed to go to the South Seas but was divinely guided to India, where he translated the Bible into over forty languages found in that country.

David Livingstone planned to go to China, but God led him to Africa as a missionary and an explorer. There he brought the blessings of salvation in Messiah to the lives of thousands. God providentially leads those who faithfully seek His grace. This grace is sometimes seen only by the eyes of faith. Messianic friends of mine in Atlanta, Georgia, needed $30,000 the next day for an outreach facility, so they prayed about it. The very next day, when they needed the money, two checks came in the mail from two different people in two different parts of the world. Yes, the two checks added up to exactly $30,000. These two checks were sent out before my friends were ever aware of the need they would have.

Providentially, grace prepares the way even before we start seeking faith in Messiah. As soon as we by faith seek grace and find it, we can walk in the good works that were prepared beforehand for us. Your life in Him depends on the fact of God's providence because "we are His workmanship, created in Messiah Yeshua for good works, which God prepared beforehand, that we should walk in them" (Ephesians 2:10).

The providence of God uses our faith in Messiah to guide us even in our mundane activities for His eternal purposes. We can faithfully work to feed our family, raise the kids, go to school – God is at work in and through us. We can trust God, because His grace guides us even as we seek His grace for our lives. A man accidentally came to a congregational meeting I was conducting in New York.

There, he prayed to trust Messiah as his Savior and Lord. I asked how he happened to come to our service. He said he was looking for the Masonic lodge but was unsure how "Masonic" was spelled and came to a "Messianic" service by accident. Accident? I don't think so. There are no accidents with the Lord, because He cares about us, and He is overseeing His universe. Ruth did not "happened as it happened" to come to just the right field to work. God was at work.

Personally Laboring In Faith

Ruth 2:4 – Now behold, Boaz came from Bethlehem and said to the reapers, "May the LORD be with you." And they said to him, "May the LORD bless you.

The story starts to develop its "love story" about Boaz and Ruth while Ruth is laboring as a gleaner. Some might not think that to be a particularly romantic setting, but this historical account reminds us that it is not the setting but the grace of God that is our sufficiency (2 Corinthians 12:9). If we closely examine the setting, we will see it as the dark backdrop on which this diamond of grace, Ruth's faith, is best displayed.

We need to remember while we labor that God is also at work. Now a new dynamic of God's gracious providence is revealed. The text states, "Now behold, Boaz came from Bethlehem." Boaz arrives on the scene. But why the word "behold"? It is expressed as if no other issues of spiritual consequence had transpired, so it seems as if Boaz's arrival was immediately on the heels of Ruth entering the field, though it is hours later.

The word *bo* again is essential: just as Ruth providentially came (*bo*) to the field, so Boaz providentially came (*bo*) back to his field. God was bringing it all together in His timing. It was not by Ruth's or Boaz's planning. This is unlike the many machinations and manipulations of our lives, such as: "Let me do this to get my spouse to love me" or "Let me do this so people will think better of me." Ministry fulfills the responsibilities God has assigned to us; manipulation tries to do a work that God never assigned.

We are just to walk by faith in the revealed will of God and leave all the results to Him. Boaz said to the reapers, "May the LORD be with you." Boaz was the boss, the owner of the field, and he blessed his workers. Fellowship at work should be at the initiative of a believing boss with believing workers. Leaders should model faith in all they say and do (Hebrews 13:7).

Boaz blessed his workers with his use of "The Name" translated here as LORD. This name of the Lord, *YHVH*, is sometimes transliterated Yahweh or Jehovah. The exact pronunciation has been lost over the years, because religious leaders determined early on that since we are not to take His Name in vain, not using it at all would assure it was never used in vain. And so by the Name's disuse, its exact pronunciation has been lost in Judaism as well as in New Covenant faith. Among religious Jews, *HaShem* (The Name) is used when referring to the Tetragrammaton, that is, the four letter name of God (*YHVH*). We should never use His name in vain or foolishly, but it is not a vain thing to sincerely desire His name to be honored in the lives of those believers around us as long as our actions prove that our devotion to Him is not merely words.

Boaz's actions showed that God was in his heart. In the *Midrashim* (Rabbinical commentaries on the Scriptures), Boaz's greeting was understood to establish a precedent in the book of Ruth:

> Ruth Rabbah 4:4 —And Boaz and his court arose and instituted that greeting should be by the name of God, as it is said, and behold, Boaz came from Bethlehem, and said unto the reapers: the LORD be with you.

A Testimony Of Works While At Work

> Ruth 2:5-7 —Then Boaz said to his servant who was in charge of the reapers, "Whose young woman is this?" 6 The servant in charge of the reapers replied, "She is the young Moabite woman who returned with Naomi from the land of Moab. 7 And she said, 'Please let me glean and gather after the reapers among the sheaves.' Thus she came and has remained from the morning until now; she has been sitting in the house for a little while."

Boaz noticed a new worker in his field. Who was that new girl? He knew his workers well enough to know when a new person, even a gleaner, had come into his field. Boaz showed good stewardship in this matter. He had heard of Ruth while in Bethlehem but had never met her (Ruth 2:11). He had heard interesting things about her life, her faith in God, and her faithfulness and loyalty to her mother-in-law.

In Ruth 2:6, the reapers responded by identifying Ruth by her ethnicity, a young Moabite woman. In that world, who cared about the names of gleaners, who were like itinerate beggars?

Ruth was not just another temporary worker, she was there to stay. In Ruth 2:7, Boaz's manager may not have caught her name, but he recognized her work ethic. We see in his report to Boaz regarding Ruth a number of qualities that demonstrated her faith that evidently impressed him.

Her humble attitude about work demonstrated faith that God's grace was sufficient. She said, "Please let me glean and gather after the reapers among the sheaves." This word "please" is the same Hebrew word, *nah*, as in Ruth 2:2, when Ruth asked Naomi for permission to go and glean. Here she also makes a courteous request of reapers for permission to glean. Jewish law more than allowed her to glean, so why would she ask? The field's owner alone could grant the privilege to glean grain from among his sheaves. Likewise, the privileges and promises of the Scriptures cannot be used as an excuse for arrogance or a demanding attitude. There is never room for arrogance with grace. One can tell if another is seeking grace by their humble attitude, which is a fruit of the Spirit and which reveals the character of our God and reflects Messiah's humble, sacrificial service for us (see Philippians 2:5-8).

Arrogance, on the other hand, shows a self-orientation and self-dependence which brings chastening, not blessing. The desire for grace recognizes that I cannot do it by my own effort. I need what God alone can provide, even if He provides that all-sufficient grace through others. Ruth was humbly sowing by faith and would reap a blessing by grace.

Her hardy activity demonstrated her faith that God's grace was sufficient. "Let me glean and gather," she had asked. Faith is confidence that God will graciously provide, according to His character and word, even while we work.

Some untaught individuals might ask, "But if she had faith, why would she have to work —and work at such a grueling job as a gleaner?" Work preceded sin; we were actually created to work (Genesis 2:8, 15). Work is an expression of faith, not a substitute for faith. As we believe God, we should seek to work, for "he who does not work does not eat" (2 Thessalonians 3:10). Benevolence is not offered to lazy people, and Ruth was faithful and not lazy.

The godly qualities of faith that depend on and seek grace are seen through her service and diligence: the text says she worked "all morning." Those who seek grace out of laziness are not seeking grace but are merely avoiding God-given labor. Laziness is still a sin.

The God who created Shabbat, a day of rest, also said, "Six days you shall labor" (Exodus 20:9). As noted previously, we are not saved *by* good works, but we are saved *for* good works. Due diligence is a result of dedication to a gracious God. When Ruth said, "Your God is my God" (1:16), she also meant to "love Him with all her heart soul and might" (Deuteronomy 6:5).

Her healthy balance regarding work demonstrated faith in God's grace being sufficient. This balance is seen in the words of the foreman, "Thus she came and has remained from the morning until now; she has been sitting in the house for a little while." Literally, she "just took a little (*ma'ot*) break."

Though she worked very hard ("from the morning until now"), Ruth paced herself and was not a workaholic. This was seen as a positive quality by the manager in his report to Boaz. Ruth had reasonable faith, not overly zealous fanaticism. Is taking breaks a sign of faith?

God created breaks, such as Shabbat. Even Yeshua taught His followers to come apart, before they fall apart. Ruth's life was in God's hands. She was complete in Him. Therefore, she did not see her life fulfilled in her labor. Ruth, like Paul, could say, "I am what I am by the grace of God." Sin, which separates us from God, makes us feel or think that we have to fulfill our lives by our own efforts. Messiah, however, came to remove sin's control over our lives. Therefore, we start out fulfilled and work in order to live out His grace, love, and life.

Ruth worked in a measured manner. Faith believes God for the Shabbat rest as well as for the week's work. Those who do not go to worship because their business demands preclude it or their kids' little league meets during worship services, not only have the wrong priorities, but also are teaching the wrong priorities to their kids. This imbalance is not a testimony to anyone.

Before coming to faith, I worked with a believer who had a sterling testimony: morally upright, joyous, content, never complained, worked, and rested without getting drunk (unlike the rest of us). I asked him, "What's your secret?" He simply replied, "Jesus." What a testimony! This guy was one of the witnesses that God used along the way to bring me to Himself. In our work as a "gleaner," mother, lawyer, or salesman, are we, too, living out the balance of faith through works that testify to those around us?

Before the days of modern navigational aids, a traveler crossed the Atlantic in a boat equipped with two compasses. One was fixed to the deck where the man at the wheel could see it. The other compass was fastened up on one of the masts, and often a sailor would be seen climbing up to inspect it. A passenger asked the captain, "Why do you have two compasses?" "This is an iron vessel," replied the captain, "and the compass on the deck is often affected by its surroundings. Such is not the case with the compass at the masthead. That one is above the influence. We steer by the compass above." Do we do the same as believers?

Or are we so caught up with all that is happening on the decks that we lose course while at work?

Maybe we are trying to do too much and too soon. Rather, like Ruth, we need to take smaller steps. A little glowworm takes steps so small that they can hardly be measured, but as it moves across the fields at midnight, there is just enough light in its glow to light the step ahead, and so as it moves forward it always moves in the light. Let us never move ahead of His light as we, by faith, seek His grace to bring glory to His Name.

In this portion of Ruth, we see through her diligence in seeking to "find grace" that faith in God walks through doors that the grace of God has opened.

CHAPTER 5

GRACE THAT OVERFLOWS

GRACE FOR THE FAITHFUL SERVANT

Ruth 2:8-9 —Then Boaz said to Ruth, "Listen carefully, my daughter. Do not go to glean in another field; furthermore, do not go on from this one, but stay here with my maids. 9 Let your eyes be on the field which they reap, and go after them. Indeed, I have commanded the servants not to touch you. When you are thirsty, go to the water jars and drink from what the servants draw."

As a Moabite, Ruth was not thought to be legal, let alone accepted, in some eyes. She was a gleaner, a day laborer — little more than a beggar. From what is taught in the Bible, I can imagine her describing her day: "We pick up grains of barley left behind by the reapers. We had to wait until the reapers were finished. We try to keep our distance from them — some of them look nasty. Some of the older gleaners have their horror stories to tell. As the new girl on the block, I get the least desirable spots to glean. Even so, some of the other bigger, harder, meaner-looking gleaners are eyeing my pouch of grain as it slowly fills. I hope to a get a couple of meals of grain picked up without being insulted, assaulted, or raped; that would be a very good day."

We saw in the previous chapter that favor (or grace) is not only the beginning of our relationship with God, but that it encompasses every aspect of our life.

In this small section of Ruth, we learn that unexpected and startling grace greatly helps the faithful servant. When Boaz approached her, she must have wondered, "Why would an owner speak to a gleaner? Is something wrong? What does he want from me?" And then she realized that he was being gracious.

Please note everything Boaz said to Ruth in 2:8-9. Ruth was overwhelmed with gratitude. She had sought grace (Ruth 2:2), but when she found grace, it was greater than she could ever have hoped for. It was so startling that "she fell on her face, bowing to the ground and said to him, "Why have I found favor in your sight that you should take notice of me, since I am a foreigner?" (Ruth 2:10) How was this startling grace instrumentally provided through Boaz? He recognized her faith in the Lord, and his own faith in the Lord then responded by being gracious (Ruth 2:12). His ministry to Ruth was a work of faith that vindicated his words of faith earlier in Ruth 2:4.

Like Boaz, our beliefs really are demonstrated and validated by our behavior. If we believe God is gracious, then by faith we should behave graciously.

We have an opportunity to extend God's grace to every person who crosses our path. We might therefore pray, "Lord, how do you want me to respond to, treat, or minister to this person? Lord, help me to minister to them on your behalf." Rather than wondering if it is in our best personal interest to help the helpless, we need to see it as the desire of God, and in His eternal best interest for this person. At each encounter, our faith in the Lord is revealed in our graciousness to others — and that graciousness may be startling to the people we encounter.

ASPECTS OF GRACE

Ruth 2:8 —Then Boaz said to Ruth, "Listen carefully, my daughter. Do not go to glean in another field; furthermore, do not go on from this one, but stay here with my maids.

Grace is responsible. Boaz's first words to Ruth were, "Listen carefully, my daughter!" Not a great pick up line, right? Actually, he was probably much older (as hinted at in Ruth 3:10), and spoke to her as to his own daughter. Literally, the words "listen to me" are "have you not heard?" (as in 1 Kings 1:11 and Isaiah 37:26) These words are a colloquialism for "You must listen to me!" This may not strike you as gracious, but it really is. What Boaz meant was, "This is vital and critical information you must have." Imagine saying to a first-time visitor in your congregation, "Listen, you must hear this! You must stay in this congregation and serve with the others here!" The visitor might wonder why you're making the first impression of a traffic cop.

Then why was this note of urgency in Boaz's first words to Ruth? Gleaning was difficult and dangerous work, even in the best of fields. In fact, Boaz had to restrain his own men (2:9), and that was on a farm with a godly owner. He may have known something troublesome about the other farms, since "each did what was right in his own sight" (Judges 21:25). He immediately understood her faith and her vulnerability, and felt obligated to help. In fact, he had already taken care of her safety, for we read in Ruth 2:9, "have I not commanded?" Her concerns were uppermost in his mind; her security, her danger, and her call by God. We, too, are to have an urgency in our sense of responsibility to others. I am my brother's keeper, and therefore "I am a debtor to all" (Romans 1:14-15).

Startling grace is not casual, or optional; startling grace is critical information that you desperately need to have. Even more than Boaz God knows the score. Because of sin, in God's sight you're heading for a waterfall, and He graciously throws you the rope. Take hold of the rope. He does not throw it for fun, but for salvation.

Grace is urgent. The Scriptures tell us there is only one way of salvation, and only Yeshua can save any who will believe on Him.

Acts 4:12 —There is no other name under heaven given by which we must be saved.

Acts 16:31 —Believe on the Lord Yeshua and you shall be saved.

As Boaz urged Ruth, so we, too, must understand that it is vital to respond to grace when it is offered, and to likewise urge others to believe.

The steamship Central America sprang a leak in mid-ocean on a voyage from New York to San Francisco. Another ship, seeing her signal of distress, headed toward her. Perceiving her danger to be imminent, the captain of the rescue ship spoke to the Central America, asking, "What is amiss?"

"We are in bad repair, and going down. Lie by till morning!"

"Let me take your passengers on board NOW," said the would-be rescuer.

It was night, and the captain of the Central America did not want to transfer his passengers then, lest some might be lost in the confusion. Thinking that they would keep afloat some hours longer, the captain replied, "Lie by till morning!"

Once again the captain of the rescue ship called: "You better let me take them now."

"Lie by till morning," was sounded back through the night.

About an hour-and-a-half later, her lights were missed! The Central America had gone down and all on board perished, because it was thought they could be saved at another time.

If someone were gracious to you, would you be wise enough to respond? It is vital to respond to grace when it's offered. When grace beckons, we must respond and not resist as some have (Acts 7:51). When salvation is offered to you, do not delay in receiving Messiah.

Grace is exclusive. Boaz said to Ruth, "Do not go walk to another field." Why? Let me answer that this way: the Bible tells how we know that a child is maturing — he will "refuse the evil and choose the good" (Isaiah 7:15), or as Paul puts it, "hate the evil and love the good" (Romans 12:9).

As we mature, we refuse evil. Grace tells us where not to be. The other fields were now off limits for Ruth. Startling grace limits your options to God's will, and God's will only. Once I married Miriam, all other 'fields' were off limits. They were no longer an option for me. Startling grace does not permit sin; it forbids it. Boaz told Ruth to stay in his fields, not to suppress her but to safeguard her.

God's protection of us is when we are in His will, not when we are disobedient (1 Corinthians 11:30). The more of His will He reveals to us as we grow in Him, the more responsible we are for what we have. As it says in Luke 12:48, "To whom much is given, much is required." The closer to the Holy of Holies the priests (*cohenim*) served, the more circumspectly they had to walk. Once we learn that it is wrong to steal, cheating on tests or taxes is no longer an option.

Joshua challenged Israel, "Choose this day whom you will serve! It is either the Lord or the false gods -- but not both" (Joshua 24:15). As Yeshua stated, "you can't serve both God and wealth" (Matthew 6:24). Grace excludes all ungodly options. Are you trying to work in both fields? If so, then you are not depending on grace. Repent and trust in God's grace alone for salvation and all He has for you forever.

Grace gives us purpose. Boaz said further to Ruth, "Also, don't pass over from this one." Ruth was not merely to refrain from other fields, but to continue working in this field of Boaz. Startling grace not only has you "refuse the evil," but also "choose the good."

We are not only asked to turn from evil, but to do good, for we are created to live for God. God's grace is not just to deliver us from evil, but it also encourages and enables us to live faithfully for God. Similarly in Israel's history in the Exodus, they weren't delivered from bondage in Egypt to merely "do their own thing," but in order to now live for God.

When Paul was saved, he not merely stopped persecuting believers, but started seeking to bring others to faith. Startling grace has us put off the old man in order to put on the new man (Ephesians 4:22-24). Those who stole are now to work to help others (Ephesians 4:28). Stop telling lies and start proclaiming the truth. We may wonder: what about the liberty of grace? You are now free to live for the Lord. You never have liberty to sin. Grace identifies us with the One we are living for, not the deeds we are leaving.

Grace brings fellowship. Boaz continued, "And thus, stay here with my maids." The word "stay" is the Hebrew word for cleave, unite, join, or associate. It is a strong word reflecting a strong commitment. This spoke to Ruth's heart; she was one who "cleaved" (Ruth 1:14); she was a person who appreciated and demonstrated faithfulness. Boaz was saying, "As you clung to Naomi, cling also to my maids." The word used is the same one that characterizes a faithful marriage in Genesis 2:24, "For a man shall leave his father and mother and *cleave* unto his wife."

Cleaving is a result of identifying with those who are committed to the same values and service. Real cleaving always assumes it is "with" others and, therefore represents having true fellowship.

Boaz encouraged Ruth to "cleave with" (Hebrew *eem*), as in "God with us" (Isaiah 7:14). At times, people do not seem to understand that meaningful community comes out of mutual commitment. A grace community is established by cleaving to friends in the same "field" of service with the same values.

This long-term commitment that cleaving characterizes is not understood in some places. The film director John Houston said of his daughter Angelica's latest romantic interest that "he is her eternal love for the moment." Real community by grace is never temporary; it is not two ships passing in the night, merely "hooking up" for the evening, but ongoing fellowship. You are one in the spirit with whoever you cleave to. Cleaving means spiritual unity, as Paul wrote, "The one who joins himself to a harlot is one body with her...the one who joins himself to the Lord is one spirit with Him" (1 Corinthians 6:16-17).

Our grace community, whether in a friendship, marriage, or in any partnership, is a spiritual commitment with agreed-upon spiritual values mutually held. Grace's fellowship transcends culture. Boaz's command to Ruth was startling grace. Why? Fellowship between Ruth and his maids was not permitted. Under the *Torah*, Jews were not allowed to associate with Gentiles, and Ruth was a Moabite. In the New Covenant we can observe a similar struggle. Acts 10:28 states, "You yourselves know how unlawful it is for a man who is a Jew to associate with a foreigner."

It was finally understood that God's grace that can save a Jew can equally save a Gentile, and thus, "the two become one new man in Messiah" (Ephesians 2:14-6). All believers are co-heirs and co-equals.

Boaz was saying, "Ruth, if you believe, you are co-heir and co-equal with my maids." Amazingly, Boaz anticipated what Paul later revealed: all those of faith are joined in the grace of life – we are one body in Messiah. "Ruth, if you believe, you are united with my maids." Startling grace encourages you to live out what is already and eternally true.

GRACE IS ACTIVE

Ruth 2:9 —Let your eyes be on the field which they reap, and go after them. Indeed, I have commanded the servants not to touch you. When you are thirsty, go to the water jars and drink from what the servants draw.

Active grace is focused. Boaz says, "Let your eyes be on the field that they [my employees] reap." During harvest time there were many reapers, both men and women. The gleaners were not hired; they were the poor, dispossessed, and unemployed. "Ruth, you may not know the borders, the parameters, safe areas, the choicest parts to glean, these experienced reapers do. Work where they work and don't let your eyes wander."

Grace makes you a follower. The issue of faithfulness becomes the challenge. Boaz told Ruth, "Don't even look around for where else to work. Where they reap, you glean." Startling grace allows for no wandering eye! We must focus to succeed; if we diffuse, we lose. The Scriptures exhort us to "fix our eyes on Yeshua" as we run the race (Hebrews 12:1-2). This directly impacts our most intimate relationship: marriage. Like Job, make a covenant with your eyes that you will not look on other women (Job 31:1).

Husbands and wives must keep their eyes on our God-given "field" and not even think of "gleaning" elsewhere. We must be faithful in our walk with the Lord. On Shabbat, do we live as a believer, but on Monday live by what's "right in our own sight?" We must not let our hearts be divided. We must not try to live in two worlds or glean in two fields.

Active grace is not diverted. Boaz continued, "and walk after them." Usually gleaners came in only after the reapers were finished, but she was asked to glean right after them while the reaping was going on. This was a great advantage. A wandering eye leads you to diverge from the path, but following is a result of your focus. How well you follow is determined by how well you focus. And what you are focusing on is seen in what you are following. Ruth was asked to focus upon and follow Boaz's maids. Who or what are you following? There are many who start out spiritually well, but get bored, distracted, and attracted elsewhere.

Some believers are involved with politics. It is true we do have a stewardship in our national citizenship. But conservative politics is not to be equated with conservative faith. Railing against the liberals is not the same as proclaiming the message of eternal life in Yeshua.

Active grace protects. Boaz assured Ruth, "Have I not commanded the young men not to touch you? You are protected here; people that are under my authority are commanded not to touch you." This guaranteed Ruth that she could serve without fear.

Unless Boaz had spoken to them, the reapers might have done what was "right in their own sight" — and what was "right" to them might be very wrong for Ruth.[1] As long as she stayed in his field she was safe. So also for every believer in Messiah —the safest place to be is in the will of God. This is startling grace, for when we are in the will of God, Satan can only work by permission, as with Job (Job 1-2), and with Peter (Luke 22:31). However, if we are out of God's will and in disobedience to God, we can expect nothing but the chastening hand of the Lord, and some of that will be by Satan's pawns (1 Corinthians 5:4-5).

Active grace is not prejudiced. Boaz concluded, "Drink when thirsty from where my reapers drink." She could drink along with the workers and not have to go away to draw her own water. Regarding Moabites, the Torah says: "You shall never seek their peace or their prosperity all your days" (Deuteronomy 23:6). But Boaz is helping a Moabite! In recognizing her faith (Ruth 2:12), he saw Ruth as a spiritual equal. He realized that if God spiritually quenched her thirst from the same fountain of living waters that He quenched the Israelites who believed in Him, then of course she could share in the same physical water as well. Regardless of her ethnicity or her economic status, she was a child of God and equal to all others. The ground is level at the cross. What Boaz is offering is a beautiful picture of the fulfillment that would come in Messiah: Now on the last day, the great day of the feast, Yeshua cried out, "If any one is thirsty, let him come to Me and drink" (John 7:37).

---

1 A similar promise is made in Ruth 2:15-16. Safety is emphasized in our current passage (Ruth 2:9). Dignity is emphasized in Ruth 2:15-16.

1 Corinthians 12:13 —So whether Jews or Greeks, whether slaves or free, we were all made to drink of one Spirit.

Equality is seen in our sharing from the same vessel, but *Torah* said all Boaz had to do to be righteous was to leave a little grain for the gleaners. Instead, he actively helped her. Boaz was not looking to see how little he could get away with, as if Torah were some restrictive fence. He realized that Torah set a minimum for love, not a maximum. By faith, Boaz provided beyond the Torah, just as the Torah itself pointed to Messiah and the startling grace He eternally provides (Romans 3:21).

Even though Boaz knew the Torah forbade helping Moabites, he also knew the forgiving and merciful character of God. As Torah condemned Moabites, it also witnessed to a God who loved the whole world and would give His Son to bear the sins of the Jewish people and sins of the world. Boaz was aware that the truth of God's great concern was for all people. In calling Abraham, God promised that Abraham and his seed would "bless all the nations of the world" (Genesis 12:2-3; 22:18; Galatians 3:14, 16).

By faith, Boaz saw that the Torah from Mount Sinai did not invalidate the promises made to Abraham (Galatians 3:17). Though God's blessing to the world is biblically true and Boaz was demonstrating farsighted faith, this is not always taught. Daniel is an Iranian Jewish man who came to faith in Yeshua while attending an Orthodox Yeshiva (Jewish religious school). As I studied Scripture with him, I asked him, "What are you studying in Yeshiva?"

He said they spent the whole day discussing at what point a person was no longer responsible to help someone – if they were one block away or two blocks away. "Daniel," I gently said, "you are responsible as long as you know they have a need. How far did Messiah come to help us?"

Grace goes beyond what is required, and does what is loving and kind. Boaz saw in Scripture that the character of God is gracious. Like Jonah, Boaz understood that the grace of God forgave His enemies. God does not desire "the death of the wicked," but for "all to come to repentance" (Ezekiel 18:32; 2 Peter 3:9). This grace repelled Jonah, but it inspired Boaz. This same God, with the same mercy, one day came in the flesh and bore the sins of His people. This is indeed a startling grace.

With all this grace, we may well wonder why did Boaz keep Ruth as a gleaner? Why not just give her a promotion to a reaper, or even foreman? Because startling grace, and not a better job title, is the key to Ruth's life, and ours as well. It is startling that by grace Ruth would do better as a gleaner than as a reaper.

The New Covenant encourages us in the same way in James 1:9, "But let the person of humble circumstances glory in his high position." That does not say that God wants you to remain poor, but fulfillment does not come through riches, nor is it hindered by humble circumstances. Fulfillment is found in God's grace in whatever situation we are in as 2 Corinthians 12:9 says, "His power is perfected through weakness; His grace is sufficient for us."

CHAPTER 6

THE CYCLES OF GRACE

HUMILITY AND HONOR

Ruth 2:10-12 —Then she fell on her face, bowing to the ground and said to him, "Why have I found favor in your sight that you should take notice of me, since I am a foreigner?" 11 Boaz replied to her, "All that you have done for your mother-in-law after the death of your husband has been fully reported to me, and how you left your father and your mother and the land of your birth, and came to a people that you did not previously know. 12 May the LORD reward your work, and your wages be full from the LORD, the God of Israel, under whose wings you have come to seek refuge.

Out of nowhere, Boaz gave Ruth opportunity and advantage that no gleaner (and certainly no Moabite!) had been granted before (Ruth 2:8-9). He went beyond what the Torah required, and acted graciously. The theme of the second chapter of Ruth is favor, or grace, as shown in Ruth 2:2, 10, and 13.

Ruth found unexpected grace, help, and care. As seen by Boaz' actions, unexpected grace is not just kind thoughts but is actually the help that the recipient of grace needs. To Ruth, this unexpected grace is as if she answered a doorbell and the man on the other side of the door declared, "You just won a million dollars!" How did she respond to Boaz? "She fell on her face!" She *plotzed*[2]! It threw her for a loop, and she could only fall to the ground in awe. How do we respond when God provides His unanticipated grace through an unexpected vessel? Well, that depends on our attitude of faithfulness.

Grace Inspires Gratitude

Ruth 2:10 —Then she fell on her face, bowing to the ground and said to him, "Why have I found favor in your sight that you should take notice of me, since I am a foreigner?

Some might think that since Boaz was the boss, Ruth's response showed her humility before authority and dependence upon that authority.[3] We see in the New Covenant a similar example of this humble faith-response. Yeshua had healed several lepers, but not all responded with faith.

Luke 17:15-16 —Now one of the lepers, when he saw that he had been healed, turned back, glorifying God with a loud voice, and he fell on his face at His feet, giving thanks to Him. And he was a Samaritan.

2 In Yiddish means to fall apart or down from a strong emotion.
3 For further study, this type of response to authority is also seen in 1 Samuel 25:23, 41; 2 Samuel 14:4; 2 Kings 4:38; and 1 Kings 1:16; 18:7, 39. The Scriptures consistently teach a respectful attitude before our "bosses" and all who are in authority over us (see 1 Peter 2:13-20).

Like the healed Samaritan leper, this Moabite gleaner recognized Boaz's provision as unexpected grace and not something that she deserved. Imagine if she had responded, "Hey, I'm Ruth, the star of this book!" If she thought she was deserving, even worthy in fact, she may have said, "Thanks Boaz, but where is my office? Do I get an assistant? What's the vacation policy?"

There are many people that demand that their needs be met. Instead their needs should bring them to humility, to seek God's grace, and then to respond with gratitude when they receive it. Ruth's response proved that she recognized herself as undeserving of the grace she received. We all need to realize that Yeshua is the Star, and we are the supporting cast. In truth, it's not until we actually surrender the lead role of our lives to the Star of eternity that we actually find fulfillment for our lives.

Faith responds to grace. Those that walk by faith are humbled in their response when they recognize unexpected grace. This was why Ruth fell on her face. Response to grace is always humbling. Unexpected grace is startling because it is always undeserved. Grace, by definition, is underserved favor.

Consequently what is undeserved is unexpected, and will startle you every time. If we are no longer humbled by God's grace, it is not His grace that has changed, but our attitude toward God. We can foolishly come to a place where we take God's grace for granted as if He is obligated to provide grace or, even more foolishly, we might somehow think we deserve God's grace.

This truth is reiterated throughout the Scriptures, and in the New Covenant it becomes Paul's personal response to the eternal, unexpected and startling grace in Messiah.

Galatians 2:20 —I have been crucified with Messiah; and it is no longer I who live, but Messiah lives in me; and the life which I now live in the flesh I live by faith in the Son of God, who loved me, and delivered Himself up for me.

2 Corinthians 5:15 —He died for all, that they who live should no longer live for themselves, but for Him who died and rose again on their behalf.

Faith is always to be our response to unexpected and startling grace. Are you still the star of your movie? You will never appreciate someone else's gracious help until you see yourself as needing grace. God's true blessings are always given because He is gracious, and not because He is a debtor to any of us. Neither our needs, nor our abilities make us worthy of help. We should humbly seek grace as Ruth did, and then humbly respond when we receive it. This is how faith responds to grace.

Grace responds to faith. Ruth said to him, "Why have I found favor in your sight that you should take notice of me?" Ruth was surprised that Boaz actually noticed her. The word "notice" is *nakar* in Hebrew, which means conspicuous or recognized. The verb also means to "pay attention to" or "take notice of someone", such as God's regard for the exiles of Judah in Jeremiah 24:5.

The potential danger in "showing attention" to someone is that it may result in partiality, as this same word is sometimes translated.

Proverbs 28:21 states, "To show partiality is not good." Therefore, judges are charged not to be "partial" in their judging (Deuteronomy 1:17; 16:19; Proverbs 24:23). Grace shows partiality; only judgment is fair —"the soul that sins shall die" (Ezekiel 18:4).

Grace notices those who are easily overlooked. Grace notices what might be considered by some as "nobodies." The Scriptures remind us that this is the biblical norm for how God eternally works.

The Messiah, the eternal Star Himself, was prophesied to be lowly and easily overlooked in His incarnation by His generation:

Isaiah 53:2-3 —He [Messiah] grew up before Him [God] like a tender shoot, and like a root out of parched ground; He had no stately form or majesty that we should look upon Him, nor appearance that we should be attracted to Him. He was despised and forsaken of men, a man of sorrows and acquainted with grief; and like one from whom men hide their face, He was despised, and we did not esteem Him.

Understandably, therefore, those that follow Him can also be easily overlooked:

1 Corinthians 1:26-29 —For consider your calling, brethren, that there were not many wise according to the flesh, not many mighty, not many noble; but God has chosen the foolish things of the world to shame the wise, and God has chosen the weak things of the world to shame the things which are strong, and the base things of the world and the despised God has chosen, the things that are not, so that He may nullify the things that are, so that no man may boast before God.

God actually chooses to use the "nobodies" that trust Him in order to confound the mighty who will not trust. You can be too big for God to use, but you can never be too small. Do you feel lost in the big world, in a dead-end job, in an unappreciative relationship? God sees you. He knows His sheep intimately and He cares (John 10:26). Therefore, the Scriptures continually reiterate God's great love for those that may be overlooked and thought of as unworthy of love.

Luke 12:6-7 —Are not five sparrows sold for two cents? And yet not one of them is forgotten before God. Indeed, the very hairs of your head are all numbered. Do not fear; you are of more value than many sparrows.

Grace has a startling recognition of us: like a light, our faith has us "standing out" in His sight. And like Boaz, when we are depending on His grace, our love for "the least of His brethren" is seen as we seek and care for the lost sheep, the ordinary and the easily overlooked. Grace recognizes and is gracious to all of faith. The reason why Ruth was so startled by Boaz's unexpected grace is noted in her final words in 2:10, "Since I am a foreigner?"

In other words, Ruth was asking, "Why me? I'm a stranger; I am far off from God. Why bless me?" In the Targum, the rabbinic paraphrase on this portion written approximately 100 BCE, the idea of Ruth's sense of alienation is focused on more fully.

Then she fell on her face and bowed to the ground, saying to him: "Why have I found favor in your eyes that you should befriend me, seeing that I am of a strange people, of the daughters of Moab; of a people which has not the merit to intermarry with the congregation of the Lord?

As noted above, the Torah excludes the nations Ammon and Moab from eligibility for marriage within the Jewish people, because they had denied bread and water to the Jewish people during the Exodus when the Israelites wanted to travel through their territory on the way to the land of Israel. Not only that, but Balak, the King of Moab, had also hired the Midianite prophet, Balaam, to curse the Jewish people because that was considered his specialty. In light of Ruth's response to Boaz she seems to be quite aware of these historical facts.

From an eternal biblical perspective, all of us are spiritual foreigners — all are alienated from God by sin, all considered "enemies of God" because of sin (Romans 5:10). Nevertheless by faith in Messiah, "you who were far off have been brought near, for He is our peace and the middle wall of partition has been broken down" (Ephesians 2:13-16). He graciously brings us near by simple faith in Him. Boaz was gracious, faithful and caring; Ruth was diligent, humble and appreciative. The faith of Boaz recognized Ruth as someone who was part of the same spiritual faith family.

There is a poignant story of a family separated by the 1950-1953 Korean War, who were reunited on Sunday, July 11, 2004. As an eighty-nine year old father was envisioning how his son would recognize him after those fifty years of separation, suddenly, he heard a cry in a crowd: "Father!" He saw a sixty six year old man running, and he knew immediately it was his son. With tears in his eyes, the father murmured, "Is it really you? But how did you know it was me?" His son replied, "When we were separated you said good-bye and looked at me with such love. It's your eyes, father. I always remembered the love in your eyes."

Sin has separated us from our heavenly Father, but grace can restore us. We can always find favor in our Father's eyes. The greatest family reunion is yet to come, and there are many family members we will meet heaven. We will say to each other, "I know you! You have your Father's eyes."

Grace Leads To Works Of Faith

Ruth 2:11-12a —Boaz replied to her, "All that you have done for your mother-in-law after the death of your husband has been fully reported to me, and how you left your father and your mother and the land of your birth, and came to a people that you did not previously know. 12 May the LORD reward your work, and your wages be full from the LORD, the God of Israel, under whose wings you have come to seek refuge.

The good works of faith are recognized. In response to Ruth's startled reaction to his gracious help, Boaz explained why he was so gracious. He related that all she did for Naomi was "fully reported" to him. The Hebrew for fully reported is a causative form for the word *nagiyd*, to make known. Doubling the verb makes it emphatic. In other words, she had a very conspicuous, noticeable public testimony. Ruth was being spoken about; people remarked and spoke of her service. She stood out. Is this unusual? Yes. Remember, people were living by what was "right in their own sight" — but here was someone that lived by faith in God. Faith in a faithless world is light in the darkness.

Yeshua taught that we should let our "light shine before men that men might see our good works and glorify our Father in heaven" (Matthew 5:16).

When a politician says that he doesn't allow his faith to impact his decision-making, then you can only wonder what value system does impact his decisions. What you truly believe is seen in your behavior. Other political hypocrites may try to win votes by spiritual talk without the actual walk, but such "faith" is "faith without works" — and "faith without works is dead" (James 2:20). Ruth's declaration of faith in Ruth 1:16 was validated by her faithful walk.

Works of faith will even go the second mile. Boaz further noted to Ruth, "All that you have done for your mother-in-law after the death of your husband." All that Ruth did, she did graciously. One woman was asked, "How would you serve your mother in law?" Her response was, "Medium rare!" Many might feel that way. Ruth was different.

Her faith is seen in service when there was no personal benefit, for her husband is now gone. Service when there is no personal benefit is being gracious. If you serve, help, or care for others because you will be accepted, paid back, or seen by men you have your reward already (Matthew 6:5-6). This type of service is natural not spiritual. Ruth went beyond all normal expectation: she demonstrated grace. Is your service characterized by graciousness — working with no motive for compensation? Witnessing is not just talking about Yeshua, but walking like Yeshua.

Works of faith are sacrificial. Boaz also noted to Ruth, "how you left your father and mother and the land of your birth." A faith testimony is not just what you do, but what you give up and can never do again. Ruth gave up familiarity, intimacy, and identity with her people. Faith is seen when you leave the comfort zone of family and friends and venture out into the commitment zone of God's will.

We need to depend on grace and walk by faith in God, as opposed to depending on family connections. Ruth's faith is seen in her sacrifice. She gave up her old life and now lived by faith in God. In the New Covenant, this walk of faith is characterized by Paul's declaration:

Galatians 2:20 —I am crucified with Messiah; therefore I no longer live, but the life that I do live I live by faith and in the Son of God who loved me and gave up His life for me.

Faith is courageous. Ruth demonstrated Abraham-like-faith. Abraham left his family to go to a land he had never been to before (Genesis 12:1-4; Hebrews 11:8). When someone moves to a new land, they look for their own kind — family, clansmen, or people of their language group. But Ruth was a stranger in a strange land; there was no Moabite community in Israel. No Moabite consulate to help. It was a high-risk situation. If Ruth did not have the wisdom to handle matters, there was no one to call, no one to tell her how to get things done.

Our faith takes us to where our experience has never ventured. This is because we are placing faith in God and not in our own experience. This testified strongly to Boaz, because those "under His wings" are revealed through faith. Is our faith recognizable to those around us? Does our life testify that we have sought refuge under His wings?

Works Of Faith Lead To Rewards

Ruth 2:12 —May the LORD reward your work, and your wages be full from the LORD, the God of Israel, under whose wings you have come to seek refuge.

When Boaz said, "May the LORD reward your work," he was letting Ruth know that the reward acknowledged her faithfulness to God. Boaz was saying that not only was he aware of Ruth's service, but more importantly, he assured Ruth of God's knowledge that her service was for the Lord. Like Ruth, all those who rely on grace and serve by grace are also rewarded by grace. Others gleaners in the same field may have had selfish motives, but not Ruth. She sought to help her mother-in-law and not herself.

The word that is used for "work" is *po'ahl* in Hebrew. *The Theological Wordbook of the Old Testament* gives an interesting insight on this word:

> When *po'ahl* describes man's actions or deeds, it refers to his moral acts, either positive (Psalm 15:2; Zephaniah 2:3), but more often negative: Proverbs 30:20 -wickedness; Job 34:32 —iniquity; Isaiah 44:15 —idolatry.

This may help to explain why in Ruth 2:12 the very form that is used there for "your work" is only used elsewhere for God's work (Psalm 77:13; 90:16; 143:5; Habakkuk 3:2). Ruth's work was seen to morally reflect His work, as all works of faith and grace do.

The word "reward" from the statement of Boaz in Ruth 2:12 is the Hebrew word *shalame*, which means complete, and is the same root for the more common word *shalom*, meaning peace.

The form that is used in Ruth 2:12 is translated elsewhere as "restitution" or "pay back" (Exodus 21:34, 36, 37; 22:6, 7). For example: when you owe someone because you are responsible for the loss of their animal, there is something incomplete in your relationship.

There is no peace between you while the debt is outstanding. However, after restitution has been made the debt is now cancelled and this "completes" the relationship and now there is peace between the two parties.

In a same way our sins make us debtors to God. Sin breaks our relationship with God and makes it incomplete. This is what Isaiah the prophet states:

Isaiah 59:1-2 —Behold, the LORD'S hand is not so short that it cannot save; nor is His ear so dull that it cannot hear. But your iniquities have made a separation between you and your God, and your sins have hidden His face from you so that He does not hear.

But how can we repay such a debt to God? We cannot, so God paid it Himself. He provided atonement which is final and made perfect restitution in Messiah, "for the Lord has laid on Him the iniquities of us all" (Isaiah 53:6). Therefore, once we trust in His provision we are declared right with Him (righteous), the debt paid, and we have peace with God.

Romans 5:1 —Therefore, having been justified by faith, we have peace with God through our Lord Yeshua the Messiah.

Hebrews 10:18 —Now where there is forgiveness of these things, there is no longer any offering for sin.

Now our service to God is a response of love. All that we do for His glory is by His grace. Therefore, God recognizes our faith by rewarding all who serve Him by faith. For though we are not saved by good works, we are saved for good works as we walk with Him (Ephesians 2:8-10).

The imperfect tense of the verb, *shalame* (complete) indicates what God is presently doing and as well as what He will continue to do. Boaz saw God's reward for Ruth at work through him. In other words he was saying to her, "What I am doing for you is a small part of God's reward."

When we understand that God's desire is to bless others, then we are willing to yield ourselves to Him and be His instrument of blessing. You may want to prayerfully consider: am I willing to be His instrument of blessing to those that He appreciates?

There is a simple principle about rewards: the One we truly serve is the One who will reward us. By promising to reward our work, God recognizes that we truly serve Him. As Yeshua taught, when people give alms, pray, or fast in order to be noticed by others, the attention that they receive from others for their religious activities is their reward (Matthew 6:2, 5, 16). Similarly, if are you seeking your friend's, spouse's, or children's appreciation for all you do for them, then their appreciation becomes your reward.

On the other hand, though you may not get any applause from the crowds, God knows all your sacrificial service that you are doing as service to Him, and He will reward. Some are serving faithfully in difficult circumstances. Some are working at dead-end jobs just to keep food on the table because they see their calling is to provide for their families, not merely advance their careers. The Scriptures assure us that no one will ever lose their reward. The One who hired us is the One who will reward us.

In fact, Boaz assured Ruth that God would reward her "fully." God always honors those who serve Him, "with all their heart all their souls and all their might" (Deuteronomy 6:5). The Lord will fully repay all our sacrifice in service for Him. If we serve beyond what is expected, we will be blessed accordingly. Yeshua assures us of this same fact in Mark 10:29-30,

> There is no one who has left family or farms for My sake and for the Good News sake, but that he shall receive a hundred times as much now in the present age, along with persecutions; and in the age to come, eternal life.

By saying, "and your wages be full from the LORD, the God of Israel" in Ruth 2:12, Boaz did more than reiterate the same encouragement to Ruth. Boaz had good reason to encourage Ruth, because the character of God is involved. Not only did the reward recognize her faithfulness to God, the reward also acknowledged His faithfulness to her. God is faithful to reward His own servants, and the Old and New Covenant Scriptures assure us of this.

> Proverbs 19:17 —He who is gracious to a poor man lends to the LORD, and He will repay him for his good deed.

> Hebrew 6:10 —God is not unjust so as to forget your work and the love which you have shown toward His name in having ministered and in still ministering to the saints.

Service to others because of faith in God will be rewarded by God, for the reward reveals His faithful character. God is trustworthy.

God rewards according to what we sow. The Scriptures teach us that if we sow sparingly we will reap sparingly. Sow beyond what is required, and reap bountifully (2 Corinthians 8:6). You can not out give God, and God always gives "according to the riches of His grace" (Ephesians 1:7). "According to" means in proportion to and God's proportionate provisions come without measure. That is why believers in Messiah look forward to "a far more exceeding and eternal weight of glory" (2 Corinthians 4:17). Therefore, we have great hope in God because He is "able to do exceedingly abundantly above all that we ask or think" (Ephesians 3:20). As we faithfully follow Him, our experience proves the truth of His promise: "My grace is sufficient for you" (2 Corinthians 12:9).

All that we do for Messiah is never to be compared with the blessings He has for us in return. This is illustrated in the following story: A candy seller saw a little boy looking hungrily at the candy. "Hey, kid, take a handful." But the kid just stood there. "Go ahead, kid, take a handful!" But the boy just stood there. Finally, a little annoyed, the man puts his own hands into the candy case and took out two handfuls and said, "Here, kid take this." And the boy, with eyes wide, took the candy in his arms. Scratching his head, the man asked the boy, "Why didn't you take some candy when I asked you to?" Walking away the boy called back, "Because your hands are bigger!"

Likewise, God will not shortchange you! His hands are bigger! We are therefore encouraged, to "seek first the Kingdom of God and His righteousness and all these things will be added to you" (Matthew 6:24).

There is more to Boaz's assurance to Ruth. The word Boaz uses for wages or reward in Hebrew is *maskoret* from the root *sacar*. This word is first used in God's great promise to Abram:

> Genesis 15:1 —After these things the word of the LORD came to Abram in a vision, saying, "Do not fear, Abram, I am a shield to you; I am your shield, your exceedingly great *reward.*"

That great reward (*sacar*) for Abram is the same reward for all with the faith of Abram — God Himself. We were created in His image in order to relate to God. Therefore, only God Himself is sufficient to fulfill our lives. To be with Him is our greatest reward. Messiah Yeshua came and died for our sins that we "might have life, and have it more abundantly" (John 10:10) In Him we have all we need now and forever, even as the Scriptures assure us:

> Romans 8:31-32 —If God is for us, who is against us? He who did not spare His own Son, but delivered Him over for us all, how will He not also with Him freely give us all things?

Therefore by faith we live and graciously care for those around us. Like Ruth, live large for the Lord to be greatly blessed in the Lord.

REFUGE UNDER HIS WINGS

The word "refuge" (*chasote* in Hebrew) in the phrase, "under whose wings you have come to seek refuge" means to seek shelter, but implies having trust or confidence, dependence upon, and hope in God as a refuge, both for His provision as well as His protection. Simply put, people who find refuge are those who realize their need for protection and seek it. Because our need is so great to have God's refuge, the Scriptures encourage us to seek refuge in God.

Psalm 2:12 —Do homage to the Son, lest He become angry, and you perish in the way, for His wrath may soon be kindled. How blessed are all who take refuge in Him!

2 Samuel 22:3 —My God, my rock, in whom I take refuge.

2 Samuel 22:31 —As for God, His way is blameless; the word of the LORD is tested; He is a shield to all who take refuge in Him.

Psalm 57:1 —Be gracious to me, O God, be gracious to me, for my soul takes refuge in You; and in the shadow of Your wings I will take refuge, until destruction passes by.

Psalm 61:4 —Let me dwell in Thy tent forever; let me take refuge in the shelter of Thy wings.

Psalm 91:4 —He will cover you with His pinions, and under His wings you may seek refuge; His faithfulness is a shield and bulwark.

Many times we lean on our own understanding instead of trusting the Lord and taking refuge under His wings.

Often we underestimate God's power. His "wings" picture the place of refuge, which is the full resource for our lives!

The word "wings" in Hebrew (*canaph*) carries the idea of a corner as in Numbers 15:38. The wing is the corner of the garment, or skirt or shirt, and is pictured in a variety of ways throughout the Bible. The Scriptures picture "wings" as a provision of power, as in Isaiah 40:31, "they shall mount up with wings like eagles." They serve as a symbol of God's power during our deliverance from Egypt in Exodus 19:4:

> You yourselves have seen what I did to the Egyptians, and how I bore you on eagles' wings, and brought you to Myself.

These same delivering wings will also deliver Israel in the future during the tribulation period:

> Revelation 12:14 —And the two wings of the great eagle were given to the woman, in order that she might fly into the wilderness to her place, where she was nourished for a time and times and half a time, from the presence of the serpent.

The Scriptures also use the metaphor of wings as picturing God's power to protect from condemnation (Psalm 17:8), joy in time of trouble (Psalm 63:7), and God's healing power at Messiah's return (Malachi 4:2). In Deuteronomy 22:30, *canaph* is used for skirt meaning protection and equaling authority showing man's responsibility to protect his wife. In Ruth 2:12, *canaph* refers to God's authority to provide for and protect both Ruth and all who believe.

We see that "His wings" point to God's full provision for us under His authority. Ironically, His refuge does not keep us from problems, but enables us to properly deal with problems.

This is how the Scripture reveals the powerful results of coming under His wings in Messiah: "I can do all things through Messiah who strengthens me!" (Philippians 4:13) and "I am more than a conqueror through Him who loved Me" (Romans 8:37). Under His wings we can live confidently in Messiah.

Boaz says, "under whose wing" using the word *tachath*[4] for "under." This indicates that the provision from God is received "under" His wings, that is, by yielding and submitting to His control. When we submit to Messiah's authority we can count on His power and His protection. Why are people spiritually defeated? They do not want to come under His authority in every aspect of their lives.

In time of war, a captured French officer was once brought into the presence of the English Admiral, Lord Nelson. He went boldly up to Nelson and held out his hand. Nelson drew back. He said, "Give me your sword, and then I will take your hand." Submission precedes provision. Have you yielded to Him? Are any areas of your life not "under His wings?"

Boaz noted that Ruth had "come" (*bo*) under His wings. This form of the word "come" is in the perfect tense and means to have already come, as an accomplished fact. In the past Ruth made a decision to yield, and trust in God's powerful provision for her life. She made a faith decision and came under His wings.

---

4 This word is used in Numbers 5:19-20, 29; Ezekiel 23:5; Genesis 41:35; Judges 3:30; Isaiah 3:6 for "under the authority," "under control of."

Some might wonder, "His powerful provision is for her to glean?" The job is not the issue, but rather who you are working for. For the Scripture states,

Psalm 84:10 —Better is one day in your courts than a thousand elsewhere; I would rather be a doorkeeper in the house of my God than dwell in the tents of the wicked.

It doesn't matter what kind of job we have, or position we hold in society, whether we are poor or rich, we are all in desperate need of God's grace. He alone can truly satisfy the innermost desires of our hearts. He alone is our sufficiency. God is our Maker. Since we were created to relate to Him, therefore He is the fulfillment of our lives. Messiah longs to gather us under His wings.

Matthew 23:37 —O Jerusalem, Jerusalem, how often I wanted to gather your children together, the way a hen gathers her chicks under her wings, and you were unwilling!

Again He pleads for all to trust in Him in Matthew 11:28,

Come unto Me all who labor and are heavy laden, and I will give you rest.

Come and place faith in Him. His unexpected grace will save and enable you to serve that He may reward you as well. So let us respond according to Psalm 2:12,

Do homage to the Son, that He not become angry, and you perish in the way, for His wrath may soon be kindled. How blessed are all who take refuge in Him!

Grace for living victoriously is under His wings:

Faith receives unexpected grace...

   ...To believe the inexplicable,

      ...To see the invisible,

         ...To bear the intolerable,

            ...To overcome the insurmountable.

And all this in order:

   ...To glorify the infallible God

      ...To exalt His incomparable Messiah

      ...To proclaim His unspeakable gift

         ...To receive His unexpected grace.

CHAPTER 7

GRACE THAT SATISFIES

To Serve Is To Satisfy

Ruth 2:13-18 — May I continue to find favor in your eyes, my lord," she said. "You have given me comfort and have spoken kindly to your servant even though I do not have the standing of one of your servant girls." 14 At mealtime Boaz said to her, "Come over here. Have some bread and dip it in the wine vinegar." When she sat down with the harvesters, he offered her some roasted grain. She ate all she wanted and had some left over. 15 As she got up to glean, Boaz gave orders to his men, "Even if she gathers among the sheaves, don't embarrass her. 16 Rather, pull out some stalks for her from the bundles and leave them for her to pick up, and don't rebuke her." 17 So Ruth gleaned in the field until evening. Then she threshed the barley she had gathered, and it amounted to about an ephah. 18 She carried it back to town, and her mother-in-law saw how much she had gathered. Ruth also brought out and gave her what she had left over after she had eaten enough.

There was an article in the Louisville *Courier-Journal*:

> Though she was told that quitting her three packs of cigarettes a day would leave her irritable at first, Elsie Kennedy, a University of Kentucky professor, confides that she didn't find it that way at all. "I stayed my old sweet self," she says, "but my friends got so disagreeable, I couldn't stand them!" My friend Irv put it more simply: "I like humanity, it is people I can't stand."

God created humanity to be fully functional by faith in Him and interdependent with each other — like a body part connected through the spinal cord to the rest of the body (Ephesians 4:15-16). However, like the effects of a spinal injury in a quadriplegic, sin breaks the connection to God. And as a result, humanity's interaction becomes dysfunctional. Messiah's atonement is the connection between man and God that provides full restoration and proper functioning of humanity in Yeshua. Proper ministry to others reveals God's grace at work. Dependence on grace to minister to others means we do not have to manipulate others in order to minister effectively.

Even though things were different in the *Tenach*, especially during the period when the judges judged (circa 1300-1000 BCE), people lived by the same faith as we do (1 Corinthians 10:11, Romans 15:4); their faith anticipated what God would provide. Similarly, our faith appropriates what God has already provided in Messiah by grace alone. These early believers illustrate the very "grace through faith" in Messiah that we enjoy.

We can glean practical principles of faith from the lives of the early believers, like Ruth. Despite the fact that Ruth was different, because of her faith in God, she was blessed by amazing grace as she found great favor bestowed upon her. Ruth not only found the gracious supply, but also great contentment and satisfaction in the Lord.

Satisfying Grace Is Practiced With Others

Ruth 2:13-14 — May I continue to find favor in your eyes, my lord; for you have comforted me, and have spoken kindly to your maidservant, though I am not like one of your maidservants." 14 At mealtime Boaz said to her, "Come over here. Have some bread and dip it in the wine vinegar." When she sat down with the harvesters, he offered her some roasted grain. She ate all she wanted and had some left over.

Ruth wanted to continue in God's grace, for it alone satisfied her soul. In this section of the book of Ruth we will learn great lessons about the satisfying grace in relationship to others: satisfying grace is practiced with others, it is provided through others, and its purpose is for others.

Ruth deeply appreciated what she had received, "Though I have no rights I've been blessed by grace." We see a similar response of other believers in the Scriptures, like Miriam (Luke 1:30) and Esther (Esther 7:3), who experienced the same grace of God. The blessing given by grace is always unmerited.

The NIV translation states, "May I continue to find favor in your eyes," and reflects the imperfect verb for the word "find" in the Hebrew, which indicates a continuing present tense or a future. Ruth was indicating that she wanted to continue to find, and to depend on the grace that she had already experienced. This is similar to Moses' response to experiencing divine grace or favor in his life,

> Exodus 33:13 —Now therefore, I pray Thee, if I have found favor in Thy sight, let me know Thy ways, that I may know Thee, so that I may find favor in Thy sight.

Like Moses, Ruth found similar favor and wanted to continue in it. Grace is not like an aspirin that removes a headache and then is not thought of, or used until the next headache. It is more like the daily bread we need for nourishment. Grace becomes part of our lifestyle of faith. In the New Covenant, Paul speaks of our initial faith in Messiah as our "introduction" to the "grace in we which we stand" (Romans 5:2). Our ongoing life of faith is to continue in this grace in which we stand. You can always tell those who depend on grace. Those who truly seek and receive grace not only depend on grace, but also desire to continue in grace.

Like Ruth, all who depend on unmerited favor, look to the Master's grace for their sufficiency. When Ruth said, "for you have comforted me, and have spoken kindly to your maidservant," the word "for" (or because) is *kee* in Hebrew and means that what follows is the reason for her interest. Ruth explained why she wanted to continue in grace. Simply put, she wanted to continue because grace alone ministered to her soul.

Grace ministers comfort to the soul for past pain: Ruth acknowledges to Boaz, "You've comforted me." The word comfort in Hebrew is *nacham*. The root of the word "comfort" seems to reflect the idea of breathing deeply. Therefore, the physical display of one's feelings, either sorrow or comfort serves as consolation, which arises out of compassion.

Ruth had left family and friends and experienced the alienation that comes in a strange new land. When she and Naomi arrived in Israel, they were destitute and hungry. She understandably felt like she stood out and was different. As a Moabite, Ruth had been concerned about acceptance, not only by those in the field, but also by those in the faith.

In the New Covenant, this is seen when a Rabbi named Saul came to faith. Though later he would become the famous Paul the Apostle, at first he was infamous among believers in Messiah as a persecutor of the Messianic faith. None of the believers wanted to associate with him (Acts 9:26), until another and well-accepted believer, Barnabas, personally "took hold" of this newly-born again Paul and integrated him into the believing community (Acts 9:27). By that same grace, Boaz was Ruth's Barnabas and helped her feel accepted.

In the Scriptures, God is described as the "God of all comfort" (2 Corinthians 1:3-6). This comfort is given in the midst of our circumstances and is exactly what the soul needs to persevere through difficult trials, new challenges, and old concerns. Ruth had left all to follow God and there was understandably a sense of loss over family she might not see again, but grace comforted her.

Walking by faith might involve suffering the loss of family and friends, but God promises to comfort us: "Blessed are the mourners, for they shall be comforted" (Matthew 5:4). This is why Paul praised God for the very comfort he had received:

> 2 Corinthians 1:3-4 —Blessed be the God and Father of our Lord Yeshua the Messiah, the Father of mercies and God of all comfort; who comforts us in all our affliction so that we may be able to comfort those who are in any affliction with the comfort with which we ourselves are comforted by God.

Grace ministers kindness for the present problems: Ruth further acknowledged to Boaz that he had "spoken kindly to your maidservant." Ruth recognized that Boaz' graciousness brought kindness to her soul.

The phrase "spoken kindly" (*dibarta ahl lev*) is literally "spoken upon heart," and is a colloquial way to refer to either speaking kindly to or encouraging someone (as in 2 Chronicles 30:22, "Hezekiah spoke encouragingly," and Isaiah 40:2, "Speak kindly to Jerusalem").

Ruth appreciated not only the practical help she had received from Boaz (Ruth 2:8-9), but also the spiritual encouragement for her soul. "You've spoken to (upon) the *heart*; you did not speak to my external issues (being a Moabite, or female), but to my heart and to my soul.

In light of her present circumstances, Ruth appreciated encouragement. Life in the field was hazardous, back breaking, and intimidating to a foreign young woman. It would have been stressful and discouraging for anyone, even Ruth, to continue a godly testimony in that setting.

"Yes," she might have said, "I'm a stranger in a strange land, but grace that ministered kindness made me feel accepted by all." Those who find spiritual encouragement to the soul are enabled to serve. To continue in grace is always a spiritual matter of the heart. God's grace alone encourages our soul to "press on to the mark of our high calling" in the Lord (Philippians 3:14).

To summarize: The God of all comfort can minister comfort to the hurting heart, and His everlasting kindness can minister acceptance and encouragement to the anxious. From the book of Ruth, we see grace overcoming two things that keep us from moving forward: 1) looking back and grieving over a past loss or sacrifice, and 2) feeling inadequate or intimidated about what's present. Both are met in Messiah's grace.

Grace is shared: Ruth shared with Naomi the comfort she received from Boaz (Ruth 2:18). When we receive God's grace we will want to share with others. We must all strive to reach out to others with God's comfort. Women, do not merely socialize with women you already know, but reach out to other women in need. Men, get to know other men. "But," we might think, "that person is Jewish, African-American, Latino!" If their differences stop us, we must repent. We are not yielding to the Spirit of God that accepts that person in Messiah. We should not allow our differences stopping us from reaching out to others. Are our homes or congregations "houses of prayer for all peoples?" That is always God's desire; is it ours? Each one can reach one in love — this is the life of Yeshua made manifest. We are here to be an instrument of His grace, and a witness of His love.

The idea of words as instruments of grace is clear in the Scriptures.

Proverbs 12:25 —Anxiety in a man's heart weighs it down, but a good word makes it glad.

Proverbs 15:23 — A man has joy in an apt answer, and how delightful is a timely word.

Proverbs 25:11 — Like apples of gold in settings of silver is a word spoken in right circumstances.

In all our interactions and communications with people, the New Covenant summarizes this matter with clear guidance in Ephesians 4:29, "Let no unwholesome word proceed from your mouth, but only such a word as is good for edification according to the need of the moment, so that it will give grace to those who hear."

You can depend on it: whatever the situation, you can be God's instrument of grace to the hearts of those around you. Is this always true? It was for Boaz, but not for Naomi. Naomi had given no words of encouragement to Ruth, but Boaz spoke to Ruth's heart. Why? Naomi was the ministry for Ruth; Boaz was the enabler to Ruth. We have to know the difference between the one who is your ministry, and the one who is your minister. You may be greatly discouraged looking for encouragement from the one who is your ministry. For example: if your husband is living a life disobedient to the Lord and His Word, it will be your calling to "win him without a word" (1 Peter 3:1). It would be very discouraging to expect him to minister to you before he becomes obedient to the Lord.

Eventually, in Ruth chapters 3 and 4, even Naomi becomes an instrument of encouragement because of Ruth's consistent gracious commitment to her. Think of your various relationships: your spouse, parents, children, friends, co-workers, and neighbors. Consider in which relationships you are the minister, and in which you are the ministry. Who is your "Boaz?" Who is your "Ruth?" Who is your "Naomi?" Seek God's grace to minister His encouragement to the heart of each person He puts in your life. Pray that your words will always be as His "apples of gold."

Grace is based on the same faith, not on the same features. In Ruth 2:13, Ruth recognizes that Boaz treated her graciously, "though I am not like one of your maidservants." How could she call herself a "maidservant" and still say she was not like his "maidservants"? She was a maidservant in her attitude, but not officially. Technically she was still just a gleaner with no official recognition like his staff of servants. Ruth knew that though Boaz was gracious to her, she was not an Israelite, but rather a Moabite and she never became an Israelite. Ruth 4:10 indicates that she remained as "Ruth the Moabite."

Ruth does not lack faith, but she recognizes the world she lives in. So also in some places of the United States, if a person of color comes to faith he may not be readily accepted in some all-white churches. That is how it was for a Moabite. Boaz was not being politically correct, instead he was spiritually correct and quite ahead of his time. God only promised to bless His people (Hosea 1:9). Boaz grasped the spiritual truth that what made a person one of His people was faith, not ethnicity. Boaz understood that being Jewish does not compensate for unbelief (Jeremiah

9:24-26), but on the other hand being Gentile does not nullify spiritual acceptance, that is always by faith through God's grace.

In Ruth 2:8-12, we have read that grace gave enablement. Now we also see that grace also gives ennoblement. It gives spiritual dignity as well as spiritual ability. Through faith in Messiah we are not only children of God, but also receive the fullness of sonship. Likewise Ruth was eternally under God's wings, even though she was different. Some people have a problem with those that are different racially, ethnically, etc. God's grace knows no such distinctions: all people who believe in Messiah are equally accepted in the Beloved. Likewise, we are to "accept one another" by the same grace that accepts us. Grace turns differences into diversity, not liability. Grace provides unity without uniformity, diversity without division. Remember, grace reflects upon the Giver, not the recipient. Grace treats others according to the spiritual character of God, not according to the physical differences between people.

Satisfying Grace Leads To Unity

At mealtime, Ruth discovered that satisfying grace not only continues though diversity, but satisfying grace actually is completed in unity. Though not like the others, grace brought her into fellowship. How is this unity amid diversity demonstrated?

When the official workers gathered to eat, Boaz said to Ruth, "come here." Boaz encouraged Ruth to join them for a meal. The phrase, "come here" is literally in the imperative *goshi halom*, "Draw near to here!" This signifies coming into very near proximity.

Boaz actually says, "Come here, that you may eat of the bread and dip your piece of bread in the vinegar" (Ruth 2:14). Do not just draw near, but draw near to eat. "Eat from the bread" is singular (*haLechem*), that is, "You, Ruth, eat from the common loaf." In the same way, "dip the morsel in the vinegar" is in the singular (*bah'chometz*), that is, "You, Ruth, dip your bread into the common bowl." Boaz encouraged Ruth, "take from the same bread and bowl as all of us, and eat with the others." The book of Ruth points to the New Covenant: One loaf and one cup for all – a picture of the Last Supper. It is also prophesied in Jeremiah that King Messiah would "approach" God in the latter days on behalf of His people:

Jeremiah 30:21 —Their leader shall be one of them, and their leader shall come forth from their midst; and I will bring him *near* to Me...

Ruth desired the full grace treatment and she got it! So Boaz continued to be gracious with a call to intimacy: "draw near to here, come close."

Ruth was being told, "We may be different, but we are *not* divided." Similarly, Yeshua draws us close to Himself, and we are spiritually united with Messiah.

Hebrews 4:16 —Let us therefore draw near with confidence to the throne of grace, that we may receive mercy and may find grace to help in time of need.

The unusual Messianic beauty of this portion was not lost on Israel. In the *Midrash* (the rabbinical commentary) on Ruth 2:14 in Ruth Rabbah 5:6 we read,

The fifth interpretation makes it refer to the Messiah. COME HITHER: approach to royal state. AND EAT OF THE BREAD refers to the bread of royalty; AND DIP THY MORSEL IN THE VINEGAR refers to his sufferings, as it is said, But he was wounded because of our transgressions (Isaiah 53:5).

Jewish people throughout the ages have known that the grace demonstrated here pointed to One who would suffer and draw us near in love.

Boaz's acceptance of Ruth is highlighted: The call to intimacy is a call to spiritual nourishment for the person of faith. We see Boaz's acceptance of Ruth: By faith, you are part of us as you partake with us. The prejudice against a Moabite at that time can be compared to African Americans in the south in the 1940s. It was inconceivable for a white person to invite an African American to eat in a restaurant at the same table, and share the same loaf of bread!

The prejudice against Gentiles was evidenced in the New Covenant as well. In Acts 10, Peter needed a vision to eat with a Gentile! Paul later revealed a mystery of the unity of Jew and Gentile in Messiah (Ephesians 2-3). Boaz knew intuitively that grace makes us partakers together. Likewise we are called to "draw near with a sincere heart in full assurance of faith" (Hebrews 10:22).

Along with unity comes equality. The text states that "she sat next to the reapers." Generally, gleaners had to fend for themselves, but now she was at the table. Grace makes us equal to His servants. Ruth sat side-by-side with the reapers. She was one of the family — not in the back of the bus. In the TV show, *West Wing*, an assistant to the president, Josh, gives a note to give the okay regarding a new worker at the White House; the note simply says, "He's one of us." Similarly our acceptance in Messiah is best pictured in the incarnation. Yeshua became like one of us, when He took on flesh and blood. He suffered and was tested in all ways as we are. "He is one of us!" He understands our fears, pain, and sense of alienation because of sin. He brings forgiveness, draws us near, and declares to the heavenly host, "They are one of us!" We are accepted in the Beloved. That is what grace does for all believers, and that is what Boaz was communicating to everyone by having Ruth draw near to fellowship — "she is one of us!"

Grace Brings Sufficiency

When she sat down with the harvesters, he offered her some roasted grain. She ate all she wanted and had some left over. Notice that Boaz personally served her! Imagine the Master of the universe personally serving us. Grace brings us close to God, who loves us and personally cares for us. Messiah says in Luke 12:37,

> Blessed are those slaves whom the master shall find on the alert when he comes; truly I say to you, that he will gird himself to serve, and have them recline at the table, and will come up and wait on them.

Messiah taught that service would mark His own style of leadership in Matthew 20:28, "just as the Son of Man did not come to be served, but to serve, and to give His life a ransom for many." He has given us an example that we might lead accordingly. Great leadership is grace leadership, for it serves others.

Boaz demonstrated the kind of leadership that Messiah taught in Matthew 23:11, "But the greatest among you shall be your servant." As Boaz demonstrated and Ruth learned, grace develops greater interdependency, rather than greater independency. It is clearly pictured in the New Covenant, that by grace we are part of a "body" all attached to the head (Messiah) and all interactively caring for each other (Ephesians 4:15-16). Messiah's final demonstration of His servant leadership was displayed when He washed the feet of His disciples at the last Passover meal before His death (John 13:1-15).

Boaz profusely served her. Many Bible versions translate, "and he served her roasted grain." In Young's literal translation, however, we find "and he reacheth to her roasted corn, and she eateth, and is satisfied, and leaveth."

The word "reach" in Hebrew, *tsavat*, carries a similar idea to the word translated in Ruth 2:16 as "bundle." The Rabbis in the Septuagint have translated it as a "pile."

In other words, Boaz gave Ruth a pile of grain. He instinctively knew she would never take as much as he wanted her to have. This meal might have been the best meal she had eaten for a while. Boaz's grace was sufficient for her small faith. God's grace is not limited by your sense of need, but determined by His desire to abundantly bless you. Yeshua put it this way in John 10:10, "I came that you might have life, and have it more abundantly."

Grace satisfies not because of being Jewish or Gentile, but by the One who loves and abundantly serves you. It is not our grasp, but His grace that fully satisfies. One lesson Ruth will never forget: grace is most satisfying when it is shared with others.

GRACE IS PROVIDED THROUGH OTHERS

Ruth 2:15-16 — As she got up to glean, Boaz gave orders to his men, "Even if she gathers among the sheaves, don't embarrass her. 16 Rather, pull out some stalks for her from the bundles and leave them for her to pick up, and don't rebuke her.

Ruth was going back to work in Boaz's field (Ruth 2:8-9), and Boaz wanted to expand her opportunity as a gleaner by placing her in a prime location without any shame. He graciously gave her a privilege.

Ruth's liberty by grace: Boaz commanded his servants, saying, "Let her glean even among the sheaves" or literally "between the sheaves," that is, the bundled reaped grain. The gleaners were only permitted to pick up the grains that the reapers had missed, but Boaz commanded his men to allow Ruth to take from what the reapers had reaped. That was an amazingly great advantage for a gleaner!

It was a great liberty of grace to boldly go where no gleaner has gone before, into the very stores of the owner. This is a beautiful picture of the graciousness of our God, the true Owner of all. He wants you freely to go and indulge yourself in His abundant blessings. In Messiah we have the wisdom of God. He desires for you to have His best and welcomes you into the very presence of God.

Ephesians 2:18; 3:12—For through Yeshua we both have our access in one Spirit to the Father... in Yeshua we have boldness and confident access through faith in Yeshua.

Faith can enter the place where unbelief never could. This is further illustrated in the history of the Jewish people, who left Egypt in the Exodus, but died in the wilderness. What prevented them from entering the land of promise? They were not able to enter because of unbelief (Hebrews 3: 19). Faith alone provides an entrance into the blessings of promise.

It was only Ruth's first day as a gleaner. However, from the moment she believed and came "under the wings" of the God of Israel, she was permitted to enter, and her works merely vindicated Boaz's decision.

What if Ruth didn't believe Boaz? She would be missing out on the privilege and liberty of getting the best grain. Are you eating and living like a stranger when grace makes you family and "partakers of Messiah?" The Scripture states, "Since therefore, brethren, we have confidence to enter the holy place by the blood of Yeshua... let us draw near with a sincere heart in full assurance of faith" (Hebrews 10:19, 22).

Ruth's Dignity Preserved By Grace

Boaz also commands his workers, "and do not insult her." The word "insult" is *kalam* in Hebrew and is also translated shame, humiliation, dishonor, or guilt. It is the shame like a father spitting in your face (Numbers 12:14), or the shame of a bully humiliating you (Judges 18:7), or the shame of being publicly dishonored (1 Samuel 20:34). Boaz did not want Ruth to experience any shame.

Since she lived in the time, where "each did what was right in his own eyes" she lived in constant danger of being insulted (Judges 21:25). When we testify that we enter into the very presence of God by grace, we can be persecuted. This truth is reiterated in 2 Timothy 3:12, "Indeed, all who desire to live godly in Messiah Yeshua will be persecuted." Indeed, we can be "despised and rejected of men" just like Messiah whom we follow.

Satan is "the accuser of the brethren" (Revelation 12:10; Zechariah 3:1). His accusations discourage believers, and despise the grace of God by which believers are accepted. Beware of being Satan's pawn rather than God's instrument of grace.

Words can be either an instrument of grace or an instrument of disgrace. Without God's grace, relationships can be brutal, but with God's grace we can encourage and esteem others in order to honor the Owner of the field.

You can imagine the laborers' finding reasons to insult Ruth: "She is a Moabite! She's just a gleaner!" To assure Ruth's safety Boaz spoke directly to the workers, not through the overseer (Ruth 2:5). "Make no mistake about this matter — do not insult Ruth. Do you think I treated her graciously to have my servants treat her disgracefully?"

Why were the reapers ordered not to insult Ruth? Because insulting Ruth insulted Boaz's grace that accepted her. Boaz was saying, "In light of how I treated her, you also treat her graciously." We are never to treat someone despicably that Messiah has treated graciously — it demeans and despises His grace.

God promises, "Whoever believes in Yeshua will not be put to shame" (Romans 10:11). We are cautioned not to injure a fellow believer with our actions, "Do not ruin [those] for whom Messiah died" (1 Corinthians 8:11). There is no disgrace for those have found His grace.

Ruth's Provision By Grace Through Faith

Ruth 2:16 —[And] also you shall purposely pull out for her some grain from the bundles and leave it that she may glean, and do not rebuke her.

Her grace provision was with purpose: The Hebrew text starts off, "And also" (*v'gam*), that is, "besides all that I've already told you that Ruth is to have, I want to increase it even more." Boaz was emphasizing that he wanted the workers to clearly know that he was not finished blessing Ruth. Perhaps one of those workers even rolled his eyes and thought, "What now? Is the boss going to give away the farm?" I can understand. For most of us, it is hard to imagine just how much God not only loves us, but also wants to bless us.

In these first words, *v'gam* (and also), we catch a glimpse of God's blessings for us by grace. Ruth wisely stated that her desire was to "continue to find favor in his eyes" (Ruth 2:13). If blessing came by grace, then it was not based on Ruth getting what she deserved, but solely upon Boaz's desire to be gracious. Likewise for all believers in Messiah today, — we do not get blessed by works, but by faith that depends on His grace. When you depend on God to be gracious, the sky is literally the limit. His desire to bless us is much more than we can "hope or think."

In fact, heaven alone is great enough to fit all our blessings which are called an "eternal weight of glory" (2 Corinthians 4:17). For "eye has not seen nor has ear heard, nor has it entered into the heart of man what God has prepared for those that love Him" (1 Corinthians 2:9).

Boaz continued to direct his workers, "Also, you shall purposely pull out for her some grain from the bundles and leave it that she may glean." The phrase, "you shall purposely pull out for her" is literally in Hebrew (*shalal*), the word for "spoil" or "plunder" (Deuteronomy 20:14). But Boaz used the infinitive absolute (a sort of doubling up the verb) that makes it emphatic. Thus he says emphatically: "Pull out bundles for her!" Most versions translate, "purposely pull out" or "You must also pull out some handfuls for her," but the point would not be lost on Boaz's workers — he was being emphatic. Make sure you do this. In fact, Boaz then adds "and leave it that she may glean" —leave it, is literally "forsake them" (*ah'zav*) the very word that Ruth used when speaking to Naomi, "Do not urge me to leave (*ah'zav*) you" (Ruth 1:16). The idea is to abandon. Boaz is saying, "The bundles are no longer yours; forsake them, they now belong to Ruth."

The workers responsibility was to bless Ruth and leave the grain for her. Her response to the grain was not their concern, but Boaz's. This could be thought of as a waste, of course. The woman who poured expensive perfume on Yeshua's feet was accused of wasting money (John 12:3-8).

Did you ever think of how much sunlight is wasted in a day? Only a bit of the sun's light comes to earth to nourish our vegetation and warm us. Most of the sun's light goes off into space, unused, unappreciated, and unnoticed. God is supplying this abundant light, just so we can enjoy a small bit of it without ever thinking that He is wasting it. God's grace can be compared with the sunlight sufficient for the salvation of the whole world. Likewise Messiah's sacrifice is not wasted, for He would have been willing to go through all the suffering, agony, and horror of the cross for just one — you — without ever thinking that it was a waste. God's grace is not diminished; His strength is not lessened at all. The Lord of Glory cannot grow weary (Isaiah 40:28).

It is His glory to provide in such abundance that the amount of that grace is beyond what creation could ever utilize. He is the eternal, omnipotent, omnipresent God of all, creator and possessor of heaven and earth. Boaz was unconcerned that the bundles might be more than Ruth could use. It was his honor to bless her beyond her needs, or even beyond her ability to gather it all.

Similar to Boaz, we are to give graciously to those "gleaners" that can never give back: visiting a dying man or helping "widows and orphans in their distress" (James 1:27). It is not like the end of the movie *Saving Private Ryan*, where the dying Tom Hanks character says to the now rescued Ryan, "Be worthy of it!" The movie ends with the now older Ryan plagued with dread and doubt that he has not been worthy of the sacrifice made for him. But being "worthy of it" is not for us to determine. Why? We are never worthy of the grace we receive, and never will be.

Imagine the angels in heaven: "Oy, look at Nadler! He doesn't appreciate anything *HaShem* does for him. *HaShem* should only give it to those that are very appreciative and will prove worthy of His grace!" No. You help a baby because of its helplessness, not worthiness. Your graciousness demonstrates your love and consideration for the child. Our graciousness reflects the Lord who is gracious to us. God's grace reflects His character — even if unappreciated by us, He is eternally gracious. Let us put on the life of Messiah and be similarly gracious (Philippians 1:21).

When I was a new believer in Yeshua, I would hang out with my friend, Baruch. He was on military disability because of a wound he received in the Vietnam war.

How would he spend his free time? He would chop firewood for a needy family while they were at work, and would anonymously leave it for them. But, when asked, "Why would you do this in secret?" He would respond quoting Matthew 6:3, "When you do a charitable deed, do not let the right hand know what the left hand is doing." Baruch taught me grace by serving his Master.

Servants represent their master. Servants are privileged to demonstrate through their service the grace and values of the Master. We are not merely teaching Shabbat School, setting up chairs, making announcements, or printing bulletins –we are serving the Master. We are not merely raising children, working at a job, or running errands —we are serving the Master. So let us graciously serve in a way that represents the Master! We represent the Lord's love to others through service. Thus, *Shamashim* ("deacons" in Acts 6:3) had to be "Spirit filled" when they fed the poor —they represented God's love for the poor through their service. And so it must be for all of us. God is showing grace through His servants. Even as Messiah, "The Son of man came to seek and to save that which is lost" (Luke 19:10), likewise we are to look for opportunities to graciously help others (Galatians 6:10).

GRACE PROVISION WITHOUT PROBLEM

Boaz concluded his instructions to his workers with a further warning, "and do not rebuke her." Ruth was not to be disgraced or rebuked! A rebuke is a strong admonition and is used to check the advance, or to hinder the progress of an enemy (Isaiah 17:13; 30:17; Psalm 76:6). A wise rebuke or strong admonition is effective in the hearts of those who accept it (Proverbs 17:10; Ecclesiastes 7:5). A rebuke is meant to bring sinners to repentance (Psalm 119:21), but it is important to remember that a rebuke can only be regarding something volitional, like laziness that can be changed, not intrinsic like ethnicity, where a rebuke would only humiliate and crush the spirit.

The Scriptures teach us that rebukes must only be done with the goal of restoration (Luke 17:3; 2 Timothy 4:2). They are to be given out of love and personal concern as a warning to those that are destroying themselves with sin.

Why would the reapers rebuke or try to hinder Ruth? Because she was not only a Moabite, she also benefited from the reapers' hard work. Under Torah, gleaners could receive only what the reapers could not easily gather. But Boaz did beyond what Torah required when he implies, "Don't lay a charge against Ruth — she is doing nothing wrong by receiving my blessing. The harvest is mine and I do as I please!"

There is nothing more demeaning than for someone to make you feel like you are worthless just because you need a helping hand. Therefore, in regards to benevolence it is often stated, "for you will remember that you were once slaves in Egypt" (Deuteronomy 5:15, 15:15, 16:12, 24:19-22).

Ruth learned that grace was delivered through others as well as enjoyed with others. Even when those others like Boaz's workers needed extra encouragement to be instruments of blessing into her life, grace was still at work. The same principal works in our lives as well.

There is humorous illustration of an elderly woman who learned to praise the Lord for every blessing. Two malicious neighborhood boys decided to pull a prank on her.

"Let's get some groceries and leave them by the old lady's door. When she opens the door she'll "praise the Lord" and go to her congregation tonight to give praise to God. And when she does that, we'll stand and let everyone know that we did it and not the Lord.

So the boys followed through on their plan. Sure enough, that night the aged saint went to her congregational service to praise God for the provision of the food.

As she stood up to share God's blessings, suddenly the boys jumped up from where they were sitting in the back and cried out,

"You're wrong, old women! We put those groceries at your door!"

The women rejoiced all the more exclaiming, "Praise the Lord! He provided groceries and had the devil deliver them!"

Regardless of the means the Lord uses as an instrument of grace, let us give Him praise for the gracious provision He has for our lives.

Romans 8:28 —We know that God works all things together for good to them that love Him and are called according to His purpose.

GRACE IS MEANT FOR OTHERS

Ruth 2:17-18 —So Ruth gleaned in the field until evening. Then she threshed the barley she had gathered, and it amounted to about an ephah of barley. 18 She carried it back to town, and her mother-in-law saw how much she had gathered. Ruth also brought out and gave her what she had left over after she had eaten enough.

The narrative states that Ruth "gleaned in the field until evening." Enabled by grace she worked hard from dawn to dusk and she saw it as a blessing. As Yeshua said in Luke 12:42-44,

Who then is the faithful and wise manager, whom the master puts in charge of his servants to give them their food allowance at the proper time? It will be good for that servant whom the master finds doing so when he returns. I tell you the truth, he will put him in charge of all his possessions.

Those believers who serve the Lord diligently enjoy the blessings now and will be eternally rewarded by their Master. We read in Genesis 3:17-19 that God pronounced the "curse" that made our work produce thorns and weeds in sorrow. In contrast, when we are enabled to work by grace it becomes an opportunity to serve, whether in the field like Ruth, or in the office, or home. Ruth's hard work in gaining nourishing food encourages us as we study the Word and find God's spiritual nourishment for our souls.

When we read that Ruth took the ephah of barley we may think of her taking a loaf of bread home. Not at all!

An ephah was ten omers (Exodus 16:36); an omer was a day's food (daily bread) for one person. (Exodus 16:16) So an ephah was enough for five days of meals for the two women, or about 30 pounds, plus the leftovers mentioned in Ruth 2:14! Why so much? Boaz had over-served Ruth so that she might graciously have enough to serve others, namely Naomi. So, Ruth *schlepped*[5] and somehow carried it all as she walked into town. What a witness that must have been. Naomi saw what she had gleaned, and Ruth gave her the leftovers. Naomi's eyes must have been wide with wonder!

God serves us that we might serve others. In the Scriptures, the ministry of God is consistently like this. Regarding Messiah's miraculous multiplying of the loaves, we read, "Taking the seven loaves, He gave thanks and broke them, and gave them to His disciples to serve to the multitude" (Mark 8:6). He gave to His disciples so they could give to others. In fact, Yeshua taught that faithfulness is seen in caring for others with what we receive: "the faithful steward gives rations to the other servants" (Luke 12:42).

Yeshua says we receive so that we might give, "Freely received, freely given" (Matthew 10:8). Similarly in Exodus 12:4, it says regarding the Passover lamb that if there is too much for the home, we were to share the lamb with our neighbors. The lamb is always too much for any one home, but the home is never too much for the lamb.

Your great needs brought you to Messiah, so that through His grace you might minister to others. Grace makes you a child of God, and His overflowing grace makes you His instrument to change this world.

---

5 In Yiddish it means to carry clumsily or with difficulty

CHAPTER 8

GRACE THAT RESTORES

THE RESTORATION OF NAOMI'S FAITH

Ruth 2:18-23 —She carried it [the grain] back to town, and her mother-in-law saw how much she had gathered. Ruth also brought out and gave her what she had left over after she had eaten enough. 19 Her mother-in-law asked her, "Where did you glean today? Where did you work? Blessed be the man who took notice of you!" Then Ruth told her mother-in-law about the one at whose place she had been working. "The name of the man I worked with today is Boaz," she said. 20 "The LORD bless him!" Naomi said to her daughter-in-law. "He has not stopped showing his kindness to the living and the dead." She added, "That man is our close relative; he is one of our kinsman-redeemers." 21 Then Ruth the Moabitess said, "He even said to me, 'Stay with my workers until they finish harvesting all my grain.' " 22 Naomi said to Ruth her daughter-in-law, "It will be good for you, my daughter, to go with his girls, because in someone else's field you might be harmed." 23 So Ruth stayed close to the servant girls of Boaz to glean until the barley and wheat harvests were finished. And she lived with her mother-in-law.

Our unbelief, hardness of heart and bitter spirit don't seem to discourage the Lord at all. In fact, God just can't take the hint! The reason is that God always acts according to His nature, His will, and His promises. He never gives up on lost and alienated people. In this passage, God is seeking to restore the faith of Naomi by His grace. The vessel of this grace is God's servant, Boaz.

Ruth believed God and was therefore determined to seek His favor or grace (Ruth 2:2, 10, 13). She found more blessing than she could have ever expected. As she lived by faith, she found God's grace to be her sufficiency. In this passage, she came home to Naomi after a day's work. Like most gleaners, if she had come back with a few handfuls of grain that would have been what was expected and would have been just fine. But she came home with over thirty pounds of grain, plus leftovers from her lunch.

In Ruth 2:17-18, we read that Ruth returned home with almost two weeks supply of food. God was getting Naomi's attention. Naomi thought she had her bitter life figured out — she was doomed by God and lived accordingly. She became hardened in her misery and became a bitter and empty person (Ruth 1:20-21). Initially she was totally unaware that Ruth was her saving grace from God.

However, God's desire is to restore the alienated and God loved Naomi too much to leave her in her bitterness. Therefore, God was breaking into Naomi's world through Ruth's ministry to her. It was a famine that caused Naomi's family to disobey God and go to Moab (Ruth 1:1-2). It was the news that God was supplying food to His people in Israel again that induced her to return as the barley season started (Ruth 1:6, 22).

Therefore, it is no surprise that it was food that got her to suspect that something unusual was happening. Just when she was all set in her negativity and bitterness, God ruined everything with an attention-getting abundance. She was stunned by the abundant sufficiency. This seems to be God's M.O. (Mode of Operation).

In Acts 3, a man born lame was expecting his "blessings" from within the box of his normal expectations. God had other ideas. God not only thinks outside the box, He dwells outside the box! Did that lame man pray that day? Perhaps, but what he probably prayed was, "Oh, Lord, have someone especially generous help me today, at least enough for a meal. Amen." So hoping for a bit of spare change, he heard instead, "Silver and gold have I not, but what I have I give unto you. In the name of the Lord Yeshua the Messiah – Rise up and walk!" He was not expecting that. And that's all that God was ever planning. Why do we pray according to our expectations? That which is outside of our expectation is that which is outside of our control. It can be very unsettling to think that your own life is not under your own control. But all that God is doing and delights to do in our lives can seem "outside the box" of what reasonable people in a rationalistic society might expect.

We need to walk by faith, depend on grace, no longer live for ourselves, but for Him, who died for us. A life of grace and the values of eternity, is what God has planned for us. His grace doesn't fit into our little world of normal expectations. The blessings are greater than our faith; in fact, the problems are permitted to prove His grace alone as sufficient. Is God shaking up your world?

Naomi's Examines The Provision

Ruth 2:19 — Her mother-in-law then said to her, "Where did you glean today and where did you work? May he who took notice of you be blessed." So she told her mother-in-law with whom she had worked and said, "The name of the man with whom I worked today is Boaz."

In the 1950s classic *I Love Lucy* TV show, Lucy would do something suspicious, and her husband Desi would respond in his Spanish accent, "Lucy, you have some 'splainin to do!" Has someone come home acting differently? Is an unfriendly person now kind and forgiving? After I trusted in Yeshua as Messiah, Lord, and Savior, I returned home to New York for a visit. I overheard one family member saying to another, "What happened to Sam? He's so different!" So, ordinarily it would be reasonable to ask, "What happened to you?" Naomi asked at least that and more.

First, Naomi asked, "Where did you glean?" This should be understood as, "You gleaned all that in one day? Where in the world did you glean —a barley storage facility?" Naomi sought a natural explanation, not a supernatural one. And so, at first Naomi thought that the primary issue was "where." In her worldly thinking: "The right place: Hmmm… where could this happen?" From Naomi's perspective, coming home with that much grain was beyond comprehension and seemingly impossible.

Then Naomi asked, "Where did you work?" Naomi's surprise and skepticism cannot be hidden, "OK, maybe it's not necessarily gleaning, since there is absolutely no correlation between a gleaner's reality and your results.

Naomi continues, "May he who noticed you be blessed!" In Hebrew the word translated "notice" is also used to show partiality. In Proverbs 28:21 it states, "To show partiality is not good." Judges are solemnly warned not to be partial in their judging (Deuteronomy 1:17; 16:19; Proverbs 24:23). Naomi hinted someone might have been a bit partial to Ruth. There seems to be a double entendre in Hebrew when she said, "May he who noticed you be blessed!" When a blessing is pronounced, the word "blessed"is usually the first word, "Blessed be the one who noticed you" (Ruth 2:20). But the phrase: "May he who noticed you be blessed" carries a different sense. There is a hint of possible impropriety. This sense of impropriety in Naomi's words was recognized in the rabbinical writing, Iggeres Shmuel, where Naomi words were characterized as, "I hope his intentions were blessed and that it was not lust which prompted him to be so extraordinarily kind." This was really not as strange as it may appear.

In certain cultures, it is commonplace to use religious language without having a particularly spiritual intent, as in saying, "bless your heart," when the person has made a foolish mistake. Naomi's thoughts and suspicions were getting the best of her. At the very hint from Naomi of any impropriety, the Hebrew states Ruth "declares" (*nagad*): "The name of the man with whom I worked today is Boaz" (Ruth 2:19). Ruth was feeling "pressed to respond."[6] To Ruth, it was unthinkable and impossible that any immoral implication would ever be permitted to be attached to Boaz.

---

6 The same word is used in Judges 14:17, where Delilah kept pressing Samson to tell the secret of his strength until he could not stand it anymore and told her.

For many of us, much time is spent where we serve or work. But the crucial issue isn't where you serve, but Whom you serve. It determines everything. A good place and a bad boss makes for a bad day every day. A bad job (gleaning) and a good boss is a blessing every day.

SURPRISING RELATIONSHIP

Please notice that Ruth does not say *for* whom she worked but "with" whom she worked. She carefully uses the word "with" (Hebrew *eem*). In fact, so that there will be no mistaking the matter, the text uses the word "with" twice. After one day of work as a gleaner, she saw herself working alongside Boaz, rather than for him. His graciousness was with Ruth while she worked, even though he wasn't gleaning beside her. In the same way God's grace is with you when you are caring for the kids, involved in tedious work, or back breaking labor.

When you serve Yeshua, by grace you serve *with* Him. This is why one of the prophetic names of the Messiah found in Isaiah 7:14 is "Emmanuel," which means God is *with* us. This is the New Covenant's perspective when it states that our service for God is "working together *with* Him" (2 Corinthians 6:1).

He is eternal, and He is *with* us forever. This gracious love is why He calls us "friends" (John 15:13-15). In fact, we are assured that "He will never leave us nor forsake us" (Joshua 1:9; Hebrew 13:5).

This truth about God's grace *with* us in Messiah is beautifully written in the beloved poem *Footprints in the Sand* by Mary Stevenson:

One night I dreamed I was walking along the beach with the Lord.

Many scenes from my life flashed across the sky.

In each scene I noticed footprints in the sand.

Sometimes there were two sets of footprints, other times there was one only.

This bothered me because I noticed that during the low periods of my life,

When I was suffering from anguish, sorrow or defeat, I could see only one set of footprints,

So I said to the Lord, "You promised me Lord,

That if I followed you, you would walk with me always.

But I have noticed that during the most trying periods of my life

There has only been one set of footprints in the sand.

Why, when I needed you most, have you not been there for me?"

The Lord replied, "The years when you have seen only one set of footprints, my child, is when I carried you."

Have you trusted in Yeshua and His grace? Then He is *with* you always. And like Ruth, all your service is with Him, for He said, "I will never leave you nor forsake you," and He meant it. Ruth realized that the startling gracious provision was because of a startling gracious person, who pictured the Messiah, who loves us with an everlasting love.

Restored Through Sufficient Grace

Ruth 2:20 —Naomi said to her daughter-in-law, "May he be blessed of the LORD who has not withdrawn his kindness to the living and to the dead." Again Naomi said to her, "The man is our relative, he is one of our closest relatives."

When Ruth said, "It is Boaz." It was the most stunning piece of news of all, and it hit Naomi like a thunderbolt. Like hinges turning a door, Naomi's life turned around at the sound of that name. Naomi realized that she was not forgotten by God. It was not just an amazingly good day at work -- it was a sign of God's grace, a reminder of God's faithfulness, and an invitation to be graciously restored. The conversation would no longer be about the gift, but about the giver of the gift. Boaz was the godly side of the family. His faithfulness to God and the way God blessed him through the time of famine, made Elimelech's decision to go to Moab appear even more shameful.

Boaz was blessed during the famine, while all of Naomi's plans in Moab went haywire. Perhaps, Boaz had warned the family to trust God and not go to Moab against God's Word. In any case, while Naomi's family rebelled, Boaz trusted God and prospered through the famine. Now, this same Boaz was the one who supplied the blessing. Why? One who depends on grace becomes an instrument of grace! Naomi recognized Boaz as an instrument of God's grace and blessed him: "May he be blessed of the LORD!"

We represent God as His ambassadors. God uses people as His instruments of grace. We relate to Him in faith in order to represent His faithfulness. He uses all —some for honor and some for dishonor (2 Timothy 2:21). Those that faithfully live for Him are used honorably, but those that disobediently live for themselves are used for dishonor. When we live for God as His instrument of grace, people get a glimpse of heaven. Indeed, following God is in our own best interests. God will never walk away from us. God cares about people and is intimately involved with His universe.

GRACE FOR THE PRESENT NEED

Naomi exclaims, "The LORD who has not withdrawn his kindness to the living and to the dead." Yes, at the mention of the name Boaz, it all dawned on her in a flash: "God has not withdrawn His kindness." He has not forsaken me "the living." Though I forsook Him, He is faithful to 'living failures.' This same God, who Naomi had blamed for her sorrows, she is now blessing for His faithfulness "to the living."

Naomi immediately realizes that she was wrong to think that she was forsaken; the plan of God began to unveil before her. Do you feel forsaken by God? Through His Word, God is assuring you that He will never leave you, nor forsake you.

Isaiah 41:17 —The afflicted and needy are seeking water, but there is none, and their tongue is parched with thirst; I, the LORD, will answer them Myself, As the God of Israel I will not forsake them.

Isaiah 49:14-15 —But Zion said, "The LORD has forsaken me, and the Lord has forgotten me." Can a woman forget her nursing child, and have no compassion on the son of her womb? Even these may forget, but I will not forget you.

Hebrew 13:5-6— Let your conversation be without covetousness; and be content with such things as ye have: for he hath said, I will never leave thee, nor forsake thee. So that we may boldly say, The Lord is my helper, and I will not fear what man shall do unto me.

Because of the perfect atonement and salvation in Yeshua, God will never forsake us. Rather we have forsaken Him. As it states of the Messiah,

Isaiah 53:3 —He was despised and forsaken of men, A man of sorrows, and acquainted with grief; and like one from whom men hide their face, He was despised, and we did not esteem Him.

Yeshua was forsaken because of our sins and was our sin offering in His God-forsaken death (Matthew 27:46). Boaz's kindness was a reminder of God's faithfulness. Boaz was the instrument God used to show He had not forsaken Naomi. In this case there were no signs in the sky, or miraculous healings —just Boaz's gracious love that showed God had not forsaken Naomi. We are the instrument to tell others of Messiah and that God has not forsaken them.

GRACE FOR THE FUTURE NEEDS

Naomi concluded her blessing, "God has not withdrawn his kindness to the living and to the dead." And to the dead? Yes, God had provided not just an immediate meal ticket, but also a lasting hope. Naomi explains to Ruth, "The man is our relative; he is one of our kinsman-redeemers." Literally, "the man is near to us; he is from our redeemers" or, as she noted, "he has redeemer eligibility."

Not only near, but *goel* material!" Why would Naomi get excited about Boaz being a *goel*, a redeemer? The Hebrew word, *goel*, which stands for kinsman redeemer has special significance. The *goel* is the closest male kin (whether a brother, uncle or cousin) that should help the family at a time of crisis. All kinsman redeemers pictured Israel's true Redeemer, the Messiah.[7] God incarnate is promised to be Israel's true Redeemer.[8] This matter of Messiah as Israel's final and greatest Redeemer is found throughout the Scriptures and is also seen in the rabbinical literature. In the Talmud, in Sanhedrin, 98a, R. Johanan said:

When you see a generation ever dwindling, hope for him [the Messiah], as it is written, and the afflicted people thou wilt save.

R. Johanan said: "When you see a generation overwhelmed by many troubles as by a river, await him, as it is written, 'when the enemy shall come in like a flood, the Spirit of the Lord shall lift up a standard against him' which is followed by, and the Redeemer shall come to Zion."

The fact that Messiah, the Son of David, would be Israel's Redeemer is also taught in the Zohar, Vol. 2, 132a. and also in Midrash Rabbah: Numbers Rabbah 14:1,

The Great Redeemer who is to be a descendant of the grandchildren of David. (See also Numbers Rabbah 11:2)

Ecclesiastes Rabbah 1:28, "As the first redeemer was, so shall the latter Redeemer be."

---

7 See Isaiah 41:14; 44:6; 59:19-21; 60:15-16; 63:16
8 Isaiah 9:6, Romans 11:26-27, Hebrews 2:9-18; and Revelation 5:5, just to list a few of the references.

The genealogy of Messiah through Ruth is not only recorded in the New Covenant in Matthew 1:5, but also in Soncino Zohar, Bereshith, Section 1, Page 188b,

> There were two women from whom the seed of Judah was to be built up, from whom were to descend King David, King Solomon, and the Messiah, viz. Tamar and Ruth.

In a comment on Genesis 19:33-35 in Zohar Bereshith, Vol. 1, p 110b, "R. Simeon said:

> The underlying meaning of the words "and he knew not" is that he was unaware that the Holy One intended to raise from her King David and Solomon and all the other kings and, finally, the Messiah.

This is also seen in Zohar, Vol.1, p.93b,

> Another example is Boaz, who said to Ruth, "As the Lord liveth, lie down until the morning" (Ruth III, 13). By this adjuration he exorcised his passion, and because he guarded the covenant he became the progenitor of the greatest lineage of kings, and of the Messiah, whose name is linked with that of God.

This great hope for Jewish people, Messiah our Redeemer was typified for Naomi in the life of Boaz. Our "Boaz" has not "left off His kindness to the living and to the dead" (Ruth 2:20). If Yeshua is Israel's Redeemer, then why has not national Israel accepted Him? As Joseph was initially rejected by his brethren and finally revealed to his brethren as their savior, so Yeshua finally will be revealed to Israel as well. As Moses was first rejected by Israel and at his return to Egypt he became their deliverer, so also Yeshua, at His return, will be accepted as the Savior of Israel.

The *goel* (kinsman redeemer) pictured Messiah in the Scriptures. The *goel* had four biblical duties:

1. The *goel* ransomed his kinsman from the bondage of the foreigner (Leviticus 25:47-49). Because of sin, we are in Satan's bondage. Yeshua has ransomed lost humanity at the price of His precious blood (Matthew 20:28; 1 Peter 1:18, 19).

2. The *goel* avenged the death of his slain kinsman as a point of honor. So our Redeemer "through death has destroyed Satan, man's murderer from the beginning" (John 8:44), "who had the power of death" (Hebrews 2:14, 15).

3. The *goel* purchased back the forfeited inheritance for an Israelite; as Boaz did for Ruth (Ruth 4:3-5). In Adam, man, the heir of all things, bartered his magnificent birthright for vanity. Messiah, by incarnation, became our *Goel* and saved us from being disinherited forever (Hebrews 2:9-15). The full restoration of the inheritance is to be at "the times of restitution of all things" (Acts 3:21).

4. The *goel* is obliged to raise up a godly seed of the brother who died childless (Leviticus 25:25, 48-49; Deuteronomy 25:5-10). Likewise our Redeemer accepts us as His bride in order that we may be born again children of God (John 1:12; 1 John 3:2). And now, united to Yeshua and abiding in Him, we bear much fruit and even produce spiritual children, training them up (discipleship) as followers of Messiah (Romans 6:5; 7:6; John 15:5; Philippians 1:11; Galatians 4:19, 27-28).

In this area of raising up a godly seed, the *goel* was especially his brother's keeper[9]. But why did we have this law to raise up a seed (child) for a dead relative? It was ultimately to maintain the Jewish people as a nation.

God's faithfulness to keep Israel is seen through family members taking responsibility to maintain God's testimony of faithfulness. Ruth's first husband, Mahlon, could not have children, but Ruth could. As surely as Boaz was an instrument of God's reward for Ruth's faith, so also he was a blessing to Naomi, and all Israel. God seems to prefer choosing individuals to establish Israel that just don't have what it takes: Abraham and Sarah, Isaac and Rebecca, Jacob and Rachel. In each case, it was His grace and commitment to make and keep Israel. If God is committed to the enduring existence of the Jewish people, how dare we not be committed in our own lives?

Therefore, it became the responsibility of every member of the Jewish community to maintain Israel as a nation, and as a testimony of God's faithfulness. As Jewish believers in Yeshua we must do all we can to maintain our Jewish identity as a testimony to God's faithfulness in Messiah, even if it means restricting our marriages to a believer with a similar calling.

Boaz only had to fulfill the last two duties of the kinsman redeemer: produce a seed and redeem the land. Boaz was going to assure Naomi that there is a future. Boaz serves as a picture of Messiah, the true Redeemer of Israel and all who believe, as he represents enablement for the present and great confidence for the future.

---

9 Levir is Latin for brother-in-law; a levirate marriage is defined as a levir bringing a seed to his brother's childless widow.

1 Peter 1:13 —Therefore, gird your minds for action, keep sober in spirit, and fix your hope completely on the grace to be brought to you at the revelation of Messiah Yeshua.

All who put their trust in Messiah and received "the first fruits of the Spirit" (Romans 8:23), can look confidently into the future.

1 Corinthians 2:9 —For eye has not seen, nor ear heard, nor has it entered into the heart of man what God has prepared for those who love Him.

What He does in the present provides assurance for the future. We have no hope for the future unless we trust Him for help in the present.

RESTORED THROUGH SOVEREIGN GRACE

Ruth 2:21-23 —Then Ruth the Moabitess said, "Furthermore, he said to me, 'You should stay close to my servants until they have finished all my harvest.'" 22 Naomi said to Ruth her daughter-in-law, "It is good, my daughter, that you go out with his maids, so that others do not fall upon you in another field." 23 So she stayed close by the maids of Boaz in order to glean until the end of the barley harvest and the wheat harvest. And she lived with her mother-in-law.

Ruth offered Naomi further encouragement in relating the words of Boaz, "Furthermore, he said to me, 'You should stay close to my servants until they have finished all my harvest.'" In other words, besides all that we have now there is more opportunity for the rest of the harvest.

As noted before, the word "stay" means cleave, cling, or adhere. If I cleave then I will be blessed. Our faithful obedience can be seen through ongoing cleaving to God's grace, which is continually provided.

This cleaving is called in the Scripture by different biblical terms, such as remain or abide. God promises that if we abide in Yeshua we will bear much fruit, but apart from Him we can do nothing (John 15:5-6). So our cleaving and abiding is seen through our attitude toward the future blessed hope:

> 1 John 2:28 —And now, little children, abide in Him, so that when He appears, we may have confidence and not shrink away from Him in shame at His coming.

Our abiding in faith in the present provides the confidence needed for the future. Naomi responds in Ruth 2:22, "It is good, daughter." Naomi's new attitude is seen in her practical and positive advice to Ruth, "You go out with his maids, so that others do not fall upon you in another field." In other words Naomi says, "Stay in the one field, lest you be seen and harmed in another" (as in Joshua 2:16; Judges 18:25).

Obedience is not only the safest place on earth, but also is the place of blessing. Indeed, the safest place for us is to be in the center of God's will. Naomi's changed attitude was a result of restoration, which enabled her to fully embrace Boaz's instruction. Things begin to change with Naomi's restoration. Previously Ruth could not accept any of Naomi's counsel, for though Naomi meant well, it was all unbiblical (Ruth 1:7-17).

However, when Naomi began to embrace the God of grace, she became an encouragement to Ruth through godly counsel. After Naomi recognized that God loved her and had not forsaken her, she surrendered to His will.

At the mention of Boaz's name, Naomi made a complete and instant turnaround and placed her faith in the God of Israel, despite her previous bitterness towards Him. By repentance and faith, life changed for Naomi. Messiah came as an atonement for our sins as a visible proof that God has not forsaken us and never will. He can change us and our circumstances in a instant. Big doors turn on small hinges.

At eighty years of age, Moses thought his life was a failure and was minding his own business, (actually his father-in-law's sheep business), when something caught his attention: a burning bush. This encounter with the living God brought him back to God's service.

The eleven sons of Jacob thought their lives were miserable, because the Prime Minister of Egypt was harassing and persecuting them. They did not know that this Prime Minister was none other than their long-lost brother, Joseph. Joseph stunned his brethren with the revelation that he was alive and he was their helper, not their destroyer. This realization changed them in an instant.

Rabbi Shaul, convinced that Yeshua was not the Messiah at one time persecuted the followers of Yeshua. Suddenly, when a bright light from heaven knocked him off his feet, at that instant, he came to faith and later became the apostle Paul (Acts 9).

Just as God restored Naomi back to Himself though His gracious provision, He can do the same for you. God loved Naomi even though Naomi thought God hated her. Naomi was shocked and shaken to her core. Up to the moment Ruth returned with the grain, Naomi was certain about her world view that God had forsaken her because of her spiritual failures. The moment she realized God had not forsaken her, she yielded to God and was restored. She realized God had used Boaz, and had a great plan to secure her future.

Ruth stayed and gleaned through the harvest season and dwelt with Naomi. She not only gleaned during the barley harvest at the Passover season, but also during the wheat harvest, which occurred later in the Spring at *Shavuot* (Pentecost).

The second chapter of Ruth leaves us realizing through Naomi's eyes the greater grace of God for our lives. God sovereignly works through the lives of faithful people to restore Naomi to Himself. His sovereign grace never gives up and is able to make an eternal difference in the most bitter of souls. Faith redeems failures because grace reverses disgrace.

CHAPTER 9

GRACE THAT REDEEMS

FAITH COUNSEL FOR TRUE REST

Ruth 3:1-4 —One day Naomi, her mother-in-law, said to her, "My daughter, should I not try to find a home for you, where you will be well provided for? 2 Is not Boaz, with whose servant girls you have been, a kinsman of ours? Tonight he will be winnowing barley on the threshing floor. 3 Wash and perfume yourself, and put on your best clothes. Then go down to the threshing floor, but don't let him know you are there until he has finished eating and drinking. 4 When he lies down, note the place where he is lying. Then go and uncover his feet and lie down. He will tell you what to do."

I have found that even the best of people are in need of good counsel. As godly as Ruth was, she would miss out on some life-changing blessings unless she received the right counsel. A restored Naomi was there to help Ruth with timely counsel.

Naomi truly believed that Boaz was God's appointed man for Ruth and the appointed redeemer for the family. Therefore, she came up with a bold plan to bring Boaz and Ruth together, but Ruth needed to initiate the plan.

People of faith step out and take the initiative. Our witness can be like that as well: how many of us are waiting for the unsaved family member, friend, or neighbor to take the initiative and ask about Yeshua —when in fact, it is our responsibility to take the initiative of faith and reach out.

Sharing the Good News could be compared to asking someone for a date. Why risk rejection and embarrassment by taking the initiative, since it can be risky and intimidating. In relationships, it is usually the man who takes the initiative to ask the lady out. But in the case of the redeemer, Torah mandated that the woman take the initiative! To understand Naomi's counsel for Ruth, we will have to understand the portion from Deuteronomy 25 and the instruction on a levirate marriage.

REQUIREMENTS OF THE LEVIRATE MARRIAGE

Every Israelite was a potential *goel* to someone in the family. A *goel*, (redeemer) was the nearest relative responsible for the rescue of a family member in any kind of danger, including the danger of the extinction of the family name, because of childlessness. Israel understood the issue of redemption first hand because God had redeemed them from bondage in Egypt (Exodus 6:6; 15:13). Therefore, those who are redeemed are called to redeem others. What God had done for Israel nationally was constantly pictured in the ongoing responsibility of a *goel* on the individual basis.

The responsibilities of the *goel* were: to revenge a murder, ransom the captive, refinance the bankrupt family land, and raise up a seed. As pertained to Boaz, he would only be called upon to respond to areas of the *goel* in raising up seed and in redeeming the family land.

This work of a redeemer is explained under "the law of the levirate marriage" in Deuteronomy 25, where we learn of the obligations in both the details of the requirements as well the procedure of rejection of a levirate marriage. Many have traditionally understood the relationship of Ruth and Boaz are part of a levirate marriage.[1]

Deuteronomy 25:5-6—When brothers live together and one of them dies and has no son, the wife of the deceased shall not be married outside the family to a strange man. Her husband's brother shall go in to her and take her to himself as wife and perform the duty of a husband's brother to her. 6 "It shall be that the firstborn whom she bears shall assume the name of his dead brother, so that his name will not be blotted out from Israel.

A childless widow was not permitted to marry outside the family if the deceased's brother was nearby. This was also the teaching in the Talmud on this portion:

Yevamos 32—If a married man dies childless, his widow may not marry whomever she pleases. She first must undergo *Yibum* (levirate marriage, that is, she must marry her dead husband's brother).

1 Josephus in Antiquities of the Jews 5:332–5 and several other Jewish authorities (Gan Eden, Nashim, 13, 30; Adderet Eliyahu, Nashim 5).

The basic meaning of *yibum* is brother-in-law (*yavam*), the duty itself is called *yavumah*, and the widow is referred to as *yevamah*. In fact, scholars think that the root word came from *Ugaritic*, the language that Hebrew descended from. It means to procreate or beget, and thus, to produce a seed for the deceased brother.

The responsibility of the brother-in-law to perform this duty predated the giving of the Torah (Genesis 38:8; Genesis Rabbah 85:5). Though the marriage was considered finalized when sexual relations had taken place, the widow was bound in marriage to the *yavam* or *livir* (the brother-in-law) until that time. The offspring of such a marriage is considered the child of the deceased brother (Genesis 38:9).

Biblically, the marriage was considered actual from the point of the brother's death. From that point, there needed to be a kind of divorce (*chalutzah*, the "removal" of a shoe) to end it, but no ceremony was needed to initiate it.

Thus Boaz was recognized as having acquired Ruth for a wife from the moment he is deemed the *livir*, or *goel* (Ruth 4:10). If a husband died childless, his closest male kin was required to produce an heir with the deceased's widow in the deceased's name.

The Purpose Of The Levirate Marriage

The purpose of the levirate marriage is to preserve the name of the deceased brother so that his name would not be "blotted out." For the sake of the deceased brother, the *goel* is his brother's keeper even after the brother's death. It was a test of love. It demonstrated love for the brother, Israel, and God.

✡ If you loved your brother, you would want his name to go on.

✡ If you loved Israel, you would want your people to continue on.

✡ If you loved God, you would want His people to continue on to testify that God will not forsake His people.

Therefore, it was considered that if you love your brother, you will perform this duty. But, if you hate your brother, then you would not perform the duty.

Deuteronomy 25:7-10 —But if the man does not desire to take his brother's wife, then his brother's wife shall go up to the gate to the elders and say, "My husband's brother refuses to establish a name for his brother in Israel; he is not willing to perform the duty of a husband's brother to me." 8 Then the elders of his city shall summon him and speak to him. And if he persists and says, "I do not desire to take her," 9 then his brother's wife shall come to him in the sight of the elders, and pull his sandal off his foot and spit in his face; and she shall declare, "Thus it is done to the man who does not build up his brother's house." 10 In Israel his name shall be called, "The house of him whose sandal is removed."

What if the brother refuses to be a *goel*? The Torah states, "But if the man does not desire to take his brother's wife." The phrase "does not desire" is simply the Hebrew word, *chaphets,* which means "no delight." This is the same word Boaz uses to explain why Ruth may be rejected by another redeemer, "But if he does not wish (*chaphets*) to redeem you" (Ruth 3:13).

It is a word with a broad range of meaning and may simply indicate anything from lack of interest to an inability to get along. After the potential kinsman redeemer speaks with the woman about his lack of interest in fulfilling this duty, she initiates a charge against him. She is to go to the city gate and talk to the elders, making an official charge against the *levir* for not taking on the responsibility of a *goel*. She was to state, "My husband's brother refuses to establish a name for his brother in Israel; he is not willing to perform the duty of a husband's brother to me." If proven true, this would free the widow from her obligation to her husband's family, and allow her to remarry outside the family. Please note, though, that the charge is a refusal "to establish a name for his brother in Israel." It is the *levir's* responsibility "in Israel" that is emphasized.

Elders Investigate The Levir's Unwillingness

The elders were to take the widow's accusation very seriously and publicly investigate this matter (Deuteronomy 25:8). Yes, he may persistently refuse even with the elders summoning and speaking to him. This is the early version of "being called on the carpet" and must have been like a court scene as it was played out.

I imagine most men would not want the public hassle. If the kinsman redeemer persists in his refusal to maintain his brother's name, then the widow again takes initiative.

Deuteronomy 25:9-10 —Then his brother's wife shall come to him in the sight of the elders, and pull his sandal off his foot and spit in his face; and she shall declare, 'Thus it is done to the man who does not build up his brother's house.' "In Israel his name shall be called, 'The house of him whose sandal is removed.'"

When the levir (*yavam*) persists in refusing his duty, the refused widow is to take action in the court room of the gates of the city. The widow removes his sandal, that is, she uncovers his foot, and spits in his face, and declares publicly that this humiliation is the fit punishment for the one who refuses to do his duty.

Please note that his duty and his humiliation is not limited to his hometown, for it states, "in Israel (not just here) his name is called, "*Beit chaloots hanaal*," which means, "House of the removed sandal!" His reputation in Israel was sealed. It was like saying, "his name is least in the kingdom of heaven" (Matthew 5:19). Indeed, some in heaven will hear, "well done," but others will be called 'shoeless.'

In Genesis 38 we read about the sin of Onan of despising "the duty of a brother-in-law" to his brother Er with regard to Er's childless widow, Tamar. He refused his duty because the child would not be his, and spilled his seed. This refusal was evil in God's eyes, and Onan died (Genesis 38:10). God takes the survival of the Jewish people very seriously.

Torah literally commanded us to be our brother's keeper, as well as to "love your neighbor as yourself" (Leviticus 19:18). In other words, because God promised to keep His people it became a law of love for Israel to maintain themselves as a nation. No Jew was permitted to be the last stop of the train of Jewish survival. Torah mandated a responsibility of love to each other. If the next of kin chose not to love his brother by not producing another seed in his name, he was to be despised.

It was a test of love for the brother, Israel, and God. If you loved your brother, you performed the duty and had a testimony of being faithful to the redemptive work of Israel. The whole Torah is only understood and fulfilled by the law of love. The Torah was given to show us how to relate to God and each other, and how all relationships are fulfilled by love. That is why each Saturday morning we recite the *V'havata* along with the *Shema*:

> Deuteronomy 6:4-5 —Hear, O Israel! The LORD is our God, the LORD is one! "You shall love the LORD your God with all your heart and with all your soul and with all your might.

When Messiah said that we are to love one another as He has loved us, He was raising the bar from loving ourselves as the standard of love (as in Leviticus 19:8) to His love for us as the standard of love (John 13:34-35). This love is our witness that we are His disciples, because love fulfills the Torah.

> Romans 13:8, 10 — Owe nothing to anyone except to love one another; for he who loves his neighbor has fulfilled Torah. Love does no wrong to a neighbor; therefore love is the fulfillment of Torah.

> Galatians 5:14 —For the whole Torah is fulfilled in one command, "you shall love your neighbor as yourself."

> James 2:8 —If, however, you are fulfilling the royal law according to the Scripture, "you shall love your neighbor as yourself" you are doing well.

Why does love fulfill Torah? We can easily be self-serving and not care for others, helping them only if it helps us as seen in Ruth 4:6.

This law of love is the basis of Ruth chapters 3 and 4. This love obligated Naomi to counsel Ruth, motivated Ruth to obey, and encouraged Boaz to take responsibility as a *goel*.

The grace provided throughout chapter two (Ruth 2:2, 10, 13) enabled them to fulfill what God asked of them in chapter three. Grace was demonstrated through Boaz, the redeemer (Ruth 2:13). Fulfillment of the law of love was the fruit of that grace. This anticipated the eternal redemption and grace that Messiah our Redeemer would provide.

By faith we are "being justified as a gift by His grace through the redemption which is in Messiah Yeshua" (Romans 3:24). Torah is fulfilled through New Covenant application, since the New Covenant teaches the same righteousness from the same God (John 13:34-35). Boaz's graciousness foreshadowed the greater grace that would provide acceptance in the Beloved.

Ephesians 1:7 —In Him we have redemption through His blood, the forgiveness of our trespasses, according to the riches of His grace.

Although the Torah of Moses showed us the path of righteousness in the law of love, only Yeshua's grace enables us to fulfill the law.

John 1:17—For the Law was given through Moses; grace and truth were realized through Yeshua the Messiah.

We receive His enablement of grace by faith so that we can faithfully live out His law of love.

Faith Counsels By The Biblical Pattern

Ruth 3:1 —Then Naomi her mother-in-law said to her, "My daughter, shall I not seek rest for you, that it may be well with you?

Now that Naomi was restored to the Lord and had rest in her own soul, she wanted to bless Ruth as well. God's Word that assures us of His concern for our welfare, also encourages us to be concerned for the welfare of others. It is true that the security of our soul is evidenced by our desire to see others secured as well. There is a responsibility of faith in attaining the rest that redemption provides. As you seek grace for yourself (Ruth 2:2), you are to seek rest for others also.

Naomi says to Ruth, "shall I not seek security for you that it may be well with you." Nothing here speaks of Ruth's discontentment, but rather this counsel speaks of Naomi's long-term desire to see Ruth blessed beyond measure. In the New Covenant, we read similar counsel, "I want younger widows to marry" (1 Timothy 5:14). This "rest" (in Hebrew, *menoach*) is in the Lord. She says, "For your well being." The need for "well being" is attained as a result of *menoach*, a rest and security that God alone can supply as we follow His Word.

The Psalmist recognized that rest is a work of God in our lives: "Return to your rest, O my soul, For the LORD has dealt bountifully with you" (Psalm 116:7).

Rest does not always involve marriage, but it can certainly include marriage. When Naomi wanted to give rest to Ruth in 1:8-15[2] it was wrong, but here it is right.

2 Naomi tried to send her daughters-in-law back to Moab to find an unbelieving husband.

Why? What's the difference? In chapter one, she wanted to give Ruth rest in contradiction to Scriptures (Ruth 1:15). Now in chapter three, Naomi is seeking rest for Ruth according to the Scriptures. Advising others to do the right thing in the right way is good counsel. Good counsel always follows the Bible's teaching regardless of how strange it might seem.

Moses wanted to redeem his people; but in Exodus 2:11-15[3] his initial way was wrong. In the book of Exodus chapters 3 and 4 it was the right way, because it was in obedience to God. The end never justifies the means. We must do the right thing in the right way. This is how our salvation works as well. God wants us to be forgiven even more than we want to be forgiven. But there had to be payment, atonement, or retribution for our sins. His holiness could not allow sin to be merely ignored or winked at, but His love could not allow us to be condemned, either. So Yeshua had to die for sins, "that He might be the just and the justifier of him that believes in Yeshua" (Romans 3:26). The right thing must be done in the right way.

Yeshua teaches us how to have true rest, "Come to Me, all who are weary and heavy-laden, and I will give you rest. Take My yoke upon you, and learn from Me, for I am gentle and humble in heart; and you shall find rest for your souls" (Matthew 11:28-29).

---

3 Moses killed an Egyptian who was hurting a fellow Hebrew. The next day, when he tried to break up a fight between Hebrews, one of the fighters asked if Moses was going to kill them like he had killed the Egyptian.

Faith Counsels In Line With God's Will

Ruth 3:2 —Now is not Boaz our kinsman, with whose maids you were? Behold, he winnows barley at the threshing floor tonight.

Naomi's counsel to Ruth revolved around one person, Boaz. He was the one. For Naomi, Boaz's relationship to Ruth fulfilled the Scripture; he was the kinsman redeemer (Ruth 2:20, 3:9). Not only that, Boaz was the same one Ruth had been serving for several months. Naomi's words to Ruth were almost like this: the very one you have been serving is to be the object of your faith for even more grace.

It is the same with our faith in Yeshua. He came in the flesh that He might be our Kinsman Redeemer. If you have salvation in Yeshua, continue to keep Him as the object of your faith as you continue to grow, always looking to Him for everything.

Colossians 2:6 —Therefore, as you have received Messiah Yeshua the Lord, so also walk in Him.

Naomi continued in order to emphasize the timing: "Behold, he winnows barley at the threshing floor tonight." This was the fullness of time, the perfect opportunity. The "threshing floor" was a public place where the workers slept during the warm harvest season after the winnowing. It was an open space so that the grain could be winnowed. Winnowing is taking the beaten grain and tossing it up in the air for the breeze to blow the chaff away, while the heavier grain would fall down to the ground.

In Israel the west wind normally begins to blow about two o'clock in the afternoon and continues through the evening and into the night. It is important that the wind not be too strong or blustery, and this may explain why the evening was regarded as the best time for winnowing. Probably Boaz himself did not do the winnowing, but simply supervised his servants as they did the work.

In all likelihood, Boaz also stayed at the threshing floor during the night in order to guard it against thieves. In any case, this would be the perfect time to make contact with the right person. And as the Scripture reminds us, "how delightful is a timely word" (Proverbs 15:23).

As Boaz had just the right words at the right time for Ruth, so now Ruth can present her timely request to him as well, "Like apples of gold in settings of silver is a word spoken in right circumstances" (Proverbs 25:11).

Ruth 3:3 —Wash yourself therefore, and anoint yourself and put on your best clothes, and go down to the threshing floor; but do not make yourself known to the man until he has finished eating and drinking.

Faith encourages us to be prepared as opposed to being unprepared. As a new believer in the faith, I was anxious to get going and "jump into the pool" of service. A wise counselor quietly reminded me, "But Sam, there's no water in the pool yet!" I still needed biblical training and a bit more maturing before I would be ready to serve the Lord in leadership.

Naomi's counsel to Ruth included personal preparation and patience. Naomi told Ruth, "Wash yourself therefore, and anoint yourself and put on your best clothes."

In the Scripture, the outerwear reflects inner faith. In this regard we see that sack cloth represented repentance and mourning (Genesis 37:34)); soft clothing represented royalty (Matthew 11:8); and fine linen symbolized righteous deeds (Revelation 19:8). Ruth was *yevamah* —a childless widow seeking a kinsman redeemer to perform the duty of a levirate marriage. She was to appear in accordance with the Torah for *yevamah*. She believed God's Word and represented her faith in her attire. She lived and prepared in light of the promises. As a gleaner, she had to appear like she was ready to work in the field. Now she had to appear as a woman desiring to be wed. Remember, he could still reject her. If she went dressed as a gleaner, she would have been saying: "I'm only begrudgingly going through with this, and don't really expect to be redeemed, blessed, and helped."

Naomi also advised Ruth to "wash" thereby, expressing to the *goel* that her outward appearance reflected her inner purity. The *cohen* (priest) had to wash in the ceremonial laver before he could enter the Holy Place in the Tabernacle (Exodus 30:20). This was a symbol of spiritual cleansing before he came into the presence of the Lord.

> Isaiah 1:16; 4:4 —Wash yourselves, make yourselves clean; remove the evil of your deeds from My sight. Cease to do evil...When the Lord has washed away the filth of the daughters of Zion.

Naomi also said to Ruth, "anoint yourself." Be consecrated for service: set apart for service, like the priests, with perfume, like the "oil of the Holy Spirit of gladness" (Exodus 30:32; Psalm 48:8).

Ruth was testifying that she was set apart for service as a wife. Most women may not realize that the calling of a wife is a calling for holy service and ministry to her husband. It takes the same power of the Holy Spirit to be an effective servant in a marriage as it does to be an effective servant for the Lord wherever the Lord has called you to serve. This is how a spouse has joy in the service of marriage.

Romans 15:13 —Now may the God of hope fill you with all joy and peace in believing, so that you will abound in hope by the power of the Holy Spirit.

Naomi's final advice to Ruth: "put on your best clothes." In other words, be clothed for honor: wear the shawl or mantle (Ruth 3:9). These clothes were an outer garment that would demonstrate her modesty and cover her appropriately. She was honoring Boaz by wearing her best clothes. Ruth dressed herself to intimate that Boaz would be getting the best that she had to offer of her life in union to him, the best of her heart, the best of her ability, and the best of her very being. This provides us a great encouragement to be cleansed in Messiah, consecrated to Messiah, and clothed with Messiah. Only in Him are we giving our very best as a response of faith to the grace of the Redeemer.

Then Naomi told Ruth, "but do not make yourself known to the man until he has finished eating and drinking." Ruth was told to wait; timing is everything. Are you prepared? Good, now be patient. Abraham had to wait twenty five years for the fulfillment of the promise of a seed. Patience is always part of the plan.

Psalm 37:7 says: "Rest in the LORD and wait patiently for Him." Patience is a character trait of God and of all godly ones that trust in Him. "Love is patient" and patience is a fruit of the Spirit (1 Corinthians 13:4 ; Galatians 5:22). Those with "patience inherit the promises" (Hebrews 6:12).

> Ruth 3:4 —It shall be when he lies down, that you shall notice the place where he lies, and you shall go and uncover his feet and lie down; then he will tell you what you shall do.

Uncover his feet? By doing so, Ruth was subtly letting Boaz know that she was here on spiritual business, as a *yevamah*, and giving Boaz a subtle hint of his responsibility to redeem (Deuteronomy 25:9). Then, "he'll tell you" whether he or another will redeem you. Is this an impropriety? No, not at all. Boaz had made the first overtures in being especially gracious to Ruth during the harvest. It was now her turn to respond. But this boldness was called for by the duty the in Torah. Besides Boaz's personal interest, he had a biblical responsibility as a *goel* to redeem Ruth (Deuteronomy 25:7-10). This type of boldness was Ruth exhorting him in kindness. By uncovering the feet, she was acting in faith-obedience (Romans 1:5; 16:26).

This principle is seen throughout the Scriptures. As Moses had to grab the dangerous snake before it became a usable staff (Exodus 4:2-5). Like Moses, Ruth had to take the initiative in order to prove the righteousness of her calling. This faith is also seen in the New Covenant, where we see the bold faith of one touching the hem of Yeshua's garment to be healed (Matthew 9:20-22).

Another Scriptural illustration is the picture of salvation in the exodus story. God first divided the Red Sea, then people had to step out in faith on the seabed, trusting that the waves would not come back over them and drown them. Also when the Israelites were about to enter the place of promise on the other side of the Jordan, they needed to take a step of faith first. Joshua and the priests (*cohenim*) demonstrated their bold faith by putting their feet on the water, then the Jordan divided (Joshua 3:13-16). Believing and obeying God is walking by faith. To come under His wings for salvation (Ruth 2:12), Ruth only had to believe and confess Him as her Lord. Now to appropriate the rest that God's Word offered, she took a step of faith.

Naomi's counsel to Ruth for redemption-rest contained the same principles for all of us: follow biblical truth, focus on the right Redeemer, prepare yourself for the promise, and anticipate stepping out in faith. Yeshua came that we might have abundant spiritual life. What we find is simply this: the counsel of faith is meant to develop the character of faithfulness. This is always the eternal counsel for our lives regardless of the circumstance that we are going though. There is a remnant ready to be saved, but we need to share with them, knock on the door, and reach out in love.

CHAPTER 10

THE LAW OF LOVE

BOLD FAITH SEEKS TRUE REST

Ruth 3:5-9 —I will do whatever you say," Ruth answered. 6 So she went down to the threshing floor and did everything her mother-in-law told her to do. 7 When Boaz had finished eating and drinking and was in good spirits, he went over to lie down at the far end of the grain pile. Ruth approached quietly, uncovered his feet and lay down. 8 In the middle of the night something startled the man, and he turned and discovered a woman lying at his feet. 9 "Who are you?" he asked. "I am your servant Ruth," she said. "Spread the corner of your garment over me, since you are a kinsman-redeemer."

I like Ruth. She had courage and boldness when it mattered —in obedience to God's will. All other courage is foolishness. What are you seeking for in life? As a realist, I want to say, the best things in life are not things. And the shortest distance between two points is not the point. God has fulfillment for your soul, His rest is His gift in Messiah that is acquired by faith. From Deuteronomy 25:5-10, the levirate marriage is an aspect of the law of love and the basis of Ruth, chapters 3 and 4. This love motivated Naomi's counsel, for God had redemptive rest for Ruth -but attaining that rest occurred when she exercised faith, which was real trust in the truth of God's revealed will. Ruth sought redemption rest by the law of love, and found that bold faith attained redemptive rest. Three lessons are revealed as Ruth sought rest by her submission, service, and surrender.

RUTH'S SUBMISSION

Ruth said to Naomi, "All that you say I will do." Though Naomi's counsel may have sounded unusual, Ruth declared to Naomi her readiness. Ruth's faith was seen in her willingness to comply with the truth. Ruth understood her obligation to maintain the Jewish people through the law of love. Ruth had vowed, "Your people shall be my people." She was willing to marry even an older man to continue her husband's line and thus proving her love for Israel.

In contrast, Ruth was quite unwilling to obey Naomi in Ruth 1:16-17, where Naomi's counsel was contrary to God's will. Once Naomi began walking with God again, her counsel now reflected God's Word and His will. Therefore, Ruth obeyed Naomi as an expression of faith-obedience to God. Dads, your kids should only obey you when you instruct them to live in accordance to God's will, and not contrary to His Word.

The best value we can teach our children is that they "must obey God rather than men" (Acts 5:29). All counsel that reflects God's Word should be followed no matter how difficult it may seem. On the other hand, all counsel that contradicts God's Word should not be followed no matter how easy or helpful it might appear.

RUTH'S SERVICE

Ruth's submission was demonstrated not only in her words, but also by her works. Ruth 3:6 confirms this, "So she went down to the threshing floor and did according to all that her mother-in-law had commanded her." Submission is always seen in service. In the New Covenant, Paul speaks of the believers' "obedience of faith" which is shown by submission to God's will (Romans 1:5, 16:26). This faith-obedience is faith in action. The response of Ruth to Naomi's counsel to her, demonstrates this faith-obedience.

The victory comes from obeying His commandments. Yeshua put it this way, "If you know these things, blessed are you that do them" (John 13:17). We are warned, in fact, to not be "mere hearers but effectual doers" (James 1:23-25). Similarly, it is not the promises of salvation that save us, but trusting that God will bring them to pass. When you believe in His promises, you actually believe that He is faithful to fulfill His promises. For example, belief in the promise of Messiah's death for our sins would be vain faith if the Messiah did not fulfill the promise and die for our sins. Faith in the resurrection is vain, unless it actually happened. Like many New Year's resolutions and promises, our willingness or desire to do things is no substitute for actually doing them.

Please notice that Ruth did "according to all" that she was instructed. Full success comes from full compliance. It is the same for believers in Messiah. If we believe that "all Scripture is inspired of God" we must also believe that "all Scripture is profitable" (2 Timothy 3:16). Our maturity will be evidenced when we do "according to all" that we are instructed. Our implementation of Scripture is the proof of our faith in the inspiration of Scripture.

Ruth 3:7 —When Boaz had eaten and drunk and his heart was merry, he went to lie down at the end of the heap of grain; and she came secretly, and uncovered his feet and lay down.

Ruth was told to wait until after Boaz had eaten and laid down, so after he "had eaten and drunk and his heart was merry," she went and laid down at his feet. The phrase "His heart was merry" (*yiy'tav* in Hebrew) means literally good cheer, that is, pleased or satisfied, a state of well being, but nothing that would suggest any excess. Boaz was a man who worked hard, ate well and was ready to rest with a happy, contented heart. This contentment is the norm for people of faith (Hebrews 13:5).

Ruth waited until Boaz went to "lay down on the heap." Boaz was sleeping on a heap, or pile of some sacks of grain. The harvest was finished and the grain was beaten, so Boaz slept with the grain to protect it from thieves.[4] The threshing floor was a public place in general, but especially at the end of the harvest with all the celebration, people and whole families might be sleeping there.

---

4 See Judges 6:3-5 for more on this problem

There was not much privacy, but that was the custom. Now once Boaz had laid down, Ruth "came secretly, and uncovered his feet and lay down." This took initiative and boldness on Ruth's part. Uncovering his feet reminded him of his moral obligation and duty to redeem a relative. A relative who refuses to perform levirate must remove his shoe and bare his foot. This whole procedure was to get him to do what was expected, or face the consequences for his negligence of duty. In more modern Yiddish parlance, we call this duty *menschkite*, which is performing a duty for the family and community out of a sense of responsibility. In the Jewish community today, one of the most respectful names that a man could be called is a *mensch*, which refers to a person of reliable character.

Ruth's gentle reminder was a loving way to alert Boaz to act like a "mensch." Providing gentle reminders is something all believers should do.

When we individually and personally commit to follow the Lord, we merely remind each other of that commitment when we are involved in ministry. When we join a congregation, we commit to help fulfill its calling and then are reminded of that commitment. By reminding each other of our commitment, we "provoke one another to love and good works" (Hebrews 10:24).

Ruth's action was a "friendly reminder," like a collection agency's first letter. Their first letter is so friendly with ten boxes at the bottom, where the first box is checked off. However, each subsequent letter and checked box becomes more demanding and threatening. The Holy Spirit is something like that: first a still small voice, then He goes on to being grieved, and then to chastening the soul. As the Holy Spirit communicates with us, our well-being in Messiah is His goal. In other words, He desires to conform us to the image of Messiah. What does it take to remind us of our commitments? As we are filled with the Holy Spirit, we become His instrument of encouragement to others as well.

> 2 Peter 1:12-13 —Therefore, I will always be ready to remind you of these things, even though you already know them, and have been established in the truth which is present with you. I consider it right, as long as I am in this earthly dwelling, to stir you up by way of reminder.

It is good to remind each other of our commitments to one another in the Lord. If Boaz was a man of faith, why did he need a reminder and why did he refrain himself from approaching Ruth? The Scriptures give us two possibilities: he was old (Ruth 3:10), and there was a closer relative who was in line ahead of him in this responsibility (Ruth 3:12). Besides all this, Boaz wanted Ruth to be appreciated in the community for who she really was, a woman of great worth. With Ruth's encouragement he now saw his way clear to move things ahead. As mentioned already, this was bold action on Ruth's part. Some who do not understand the scriptural background of her initiative, would think it was indiscreet, or even quite forward. But in fact, it was biblically mandated.

At times it takes a bold step of faith to follow God's Word and take the initiative to give someone you know a "gentle reminder" of their opportunity to respond even as the Scripture teaches, and to trust in the Messiah of Israel for themselves.

Ruth's Surrender

Ruth 3:8-9 — It happened in the middle of the night that the man was startled, and bent forward; and behold, a woman was lying at his feet. "Who are you?" he asked. "I am your servant Ruth," she said. "Spread the corner of your garment over me, since you are a kinsman-redeemer."

This whole matter of "baring" his feet came as quite a surprise to Boaz. It is easy for many to be confused by the bold service of a believer, who walks according to the truth of Scripture. Is God doing something confusing, surprising, or unexpected in your life? How should you respond? In Boaz's response, we see a godly man in the midst of change. Boaz's response is the same as it should be for all of us who believe in Messiah when God surprisingly re-directs us.

Boaz was "startled" by Ruth's approach. The word "startled" is *kharad* in Hebrew and is used for being frightened (Genesis 42:28). Another usage of this word is found in Exodus 19:18, for the shaking and quaking of Mount Sinai at the approach and presence of God. Although Boaz was not exactly shaking or quaking, he was quite startled. It was a wake-up call.

"For My hand made all these things," declares the LORD. "But to this one I will look, to him who is humble and contrite of spirit, and who *trembles* at My word."

In the Septuagint we get further insight on the word "startling." Sometimes it carries the idea of "amazing," as when God does the unusual and unexpected miracle (Mark 2:12, 5:42, 6:51, Luke 2:47, 24:22).

Another example is in Acts 9:21; 10:45 when Paul came to faith in Yeshua (Acts 9:21; 10:45). For all believers, obedience to truth can be startling.

Boaz was flexible and ready to change. Boaz woke up with a startle and "turned around and discovered a woman lying at his feet." When it says "turn around" it also means "twisted around" which refers not only to the physical change of position, but also troubling to his mind and unsettling to his soul.

God desires the best for us, therefore He may at times startle us to wake us up from our complacency. God expects us to be manageable when He brings change into our life.

Boaz was focused. The text uses the word "Behold!" This is an interjection demanding our attention, "Look!" "See!" There is something to focus on that we need to focus upon. Is it the poor around us? Is it the homeless that need our compassion and action? Is it the lost sheep of the house of Israel that God continues to reach out to and He wants us to co-labor with Him?

What startled Boaz? His feet were uncovered, and a woman was there. Boaz didn't recognize Ruth immediately because he had always seen her in her work clothes. But here he sees Ruth dressed in her best clothes, laying at his feet. Then Boaz said: "Who are you?" And she answered, "I am Ruth your maid. So spread your covering over your maid, for you are a close relative." In this verse Ruth submitted to Boaz's authority as she sought her redemptive rest from her *goel.*

In acknowledging herself as his maid or *amah* in Hebrew, she defers to His will. In the book of Ruth, there are three different words for servants, *na'arim* in Ruth 2:5- 6, which means strong, youthful able workers; *shifkah* which means trustworthy family servants as in Ruth 2:13; and *amah* in Ruth 3:9, which means one yielded to the master's will, such as a slave. It is a term that is used for literal slaves (Ezra 2:65), but also by those who figuratively call themselves *amah* as an expression of humility and submission. In the Septuagint and New Covenant the Greek word is *doulos*, which a slave. This word is used commonly in the New Covenant to characterize our submission to the will of God in Messiah.

> Romans 6:16-17 —Do you not know that when you present yourselves to someone as slaves for obedience, you are slaves of the one whom you obey, either of sin resulting in death, or of obedience resulting in righteousness? But thanks be to God that though you were slaves of sin, you became obedient from the heart to that form of teaching to which you were committed.

> 1 Corinthians 7:22 —For he who was called in the Lord while a slave, is the Lord's freedman; likewise he who was called while free, is Messiah's slave.

So we are to "act as free men, and do not use your freedom as a covering for evil, but use it as bondslaves of God" (1 Peter 2:16). Even Messiah humbled Himself as a slave and was humbled even to the death on the cross (Philippians 2:7).

Ruth continued, "So spread your covering over your maid." More literally it would be read, "So spread your wing over your maid," or spread your *canaf*, which is Hebrew for covering or wing, as discussed in Ruth 2:12.

The word *canaf* (covering) refers to protection of authority (Deuteronomy 22:30, 27:20). Boaz had declared that Ruth, by faith, was under the "wings" of *HaShem*, so Ruth declared herself under Boaz's authority. Ruth realized that Boaz's work as her *goel* would bring her redemptive rest. Therefore, she submitted herself to his work. The wings of authority are spread to protect those in a covenant relationship, as God did with Israel in Deuteronomy 32:11. It is also clearly seen in Ezekiel 16:8,

> "Then I passed by you and saw you; I spread My skirt (*canaf*) over you and covered you. I also swore to you and entered into a covenant with you so that you became Mine," declares the Lord GOD.

Ruth, as a Gentile believer, is a beautiful picture of those Gentiles that by faith in Messiah, the true and eternal *Goel*, have come into a covenant relationship with *HaShem* on the basis of His mercy and grace. This fact of Gentile believers coming into covenant alongside believing Israel is clearly taught in Ephesians 2:11-16:

> Therefore remember that formerly you, the Gentiles in the flesh, who are called "Uncircumcision" by the so-called "Circumcision," which is performed in the flesh by human hands -- remember that you were at that time separate from Messiah, excluded from the commonwealth of Israel, and strangers to the covenants of promise, having no hope and without God in the world. But now in Messiah Yeshua you who formerly were far off have been brought near by the blood of Messiah. For He Himself is our peace, who made both groups into one and broke down the barrier of the dividing wall by abolishing in His flesh the enmity, which is the Law of commandments contained in ordinances, so that in Himself He might

make the two into one new man, thus establishing peace, and might reconcile them both in one body to God through the cross, by it having put to death the enmity.

Ruth was a "stranger to the covenants," but her *goel* was mercifully asked to spread his authority over her and fulfill his duty of bringing her into redemptive rest. This submission by Ruth to Boaz's authority was signified by Boaz spreading his covering over Ruth. In this way, both Ruth and Boaz signified acceptance of the levirate laws, where Ruth would be under Boaz's authority and even called by his name. The Targum on Ruth 3:9 seems to capture the same idea: "I'm Ruth, your servant. Let your name be called over your maidservant, since you're a redeemer." His name, which symbolized his authority, was called over her.

This was a legal request from Ruth to Boaz according to the intent of Scripture regarding levirate marriage. In other words, the one who redeemed her was the one who will marry her. Ruth was clearly requesting protection, with the specific meaning: "will you marry me?" In redemption, there is union and protection. There is never protection without union with the Redeemer.

In the same way when Yeshua is our Redeemer, we are His bride. We needed redemption because we were separated from God because of our sins. Likewise in our "marriage" to Messiah, the name of our true *Goel*, Yeshua is over us. In that name, and in no other name, there is salvation.

Acts 4:12 —And there is salvation in no one else; for there is no other name under heaven that has been given among men by which we must be saved.

There can be no redemptive rest unless we submit to His authority and "confess Yeshua is Lord" (as in Romans 10:9). Ruth then gave the reason for her request, "for you are kinsman-redeemer." In Hebrew it is simply, *kee goel atah*. Because Boaz was a godly man, he recognized his responsibility to fulfill the duty of a kinsman-redeemer.

Yeshua is our ultimate Kinsman-Redeemer. Why did Yeshua suffer and die for sins? Was it to become our Redeemer? No, actually it is the other way around. Before Yeshua suffered and died, He was the Redeemer, for He was "born king of the Jews" (Matthew 2:2). He did not die to become our Redeemer, he died and rose again because He is the Redeemer.

He is the Redeemer, but is He your Redeemer? He is Lord, but is He your Lord? Remember what Ruth taught us: Rest is found in the *Goel* under His authority and being yielded to His will.

CHAPTER 11

MY REDEEMER LIVES

THE TRUE REDEEMER ASSURES TRUE REST

Ruth 3:10-18 — Then he said, "May you be blessed of the LORD, my daughter. You have shown your last kindness to be better than the first by not going after young men, whether poor or rich. 11 "Now, my daughter, do not fear. I will do for you whatever you ask , for all my people in the city know that you are a woman of excellence. 12 "Now it is true I am a close relative; however, there is a relative closer than I. 13 "Remain this night, and when morning comes, if he will redeem you, good; let him redeem you. But if he does not wish to redeem you, then I will redeem you, as the LORD lives. Lie down until morning." 14 So she lay at his feet until morning and rose before one could recognize another; and he said, "Let it not be known that the woman came to the threshing floor." 15 Again he said, "Give me the cloak that is on you and hold it." So she held it, and he measured six measures of barley and laid it on her. Then she went into the city.

16 When she came to her mother-in-law, she said, "How did it go, my daughter?" And she told her all that the man had done for her. 17 She said, "These six measures of barley he gave to me, for he said, 'Do not go to your mother-in-law empty-handed.' " 18 Then she said, "Wait, my daughter, until you know how the matter turns out; for the man will not rest until he has settled it today."

In this first section, Boaz's words mirror the actions of God. Boaz said to Ruth, "May you be blessed of the LORD." He blessed her bold faith. In fact, the Hebrew carries a further aspect to this blessing. Be blessed not only of the Lord, but also to the Lord (*L' Adonai*). In other words Boaz is saying to Ruth, "God is not only blessing you, but you are also blessing the Lord." As believers when we follow the Scriptures and our lives reflect His values and priorities, then we are blessing the Lord. Psalm 103:1 says, "Bless the Lord, O my soul and all that is within me bless His Holy name."

Boaz continues to encourage Ruth, "You have shown your last kindness to be better than the first." When Boaz says "first" he is referring to Ruth's gracious concern and loyalty to her mother-in-law, and the memory of her departed husband (Ruth 2:11). Therefore her present works of faith are "better" (the Hebrew adds the concept of growing, increasing, or maturing) than her former acts of kindness. As faithful as Ruth seemed initially, Boaz recognized she was maturing. The New Covenant encourages us to "grow in the grace and knowledge of the Lord" (2 Peter 3:18). God always blesses growth that shows itself through the law of love.

Her loyalty to her deceased husband was seen in seeking a redeemer. Ruth was not merely looking for a husband, but a *goel*, in order to carry on Mahlon's name, and the name of his father, Elimelech. Ruth was obeying the law of love and demonstrating spiritual maturity. Maturity is evidenced through sacrificing for the long-term purpose of God's redemptive program.

We can learn from Ruth by the way she accepted and obeyed God's commandments and identified with Israel. Gentiles have been grafted into the olive tree by faith in Yeshua, but both Jewish and Gentile believers are called to "pray for the peace of Jerusalem" (Psalm 122:6). Our point of prayer is not only for the lost sheep of the house of Israel to come to the knowledge of their Messiah and be saved, but also that Israel will be nationally restored to God. And this national restoration will be the key to the Second Coming of Messiah.

> Matthew 23:39 —Yeshua said, "I tell you, you will not see me again until you say, 'Blessed is he who comes in the name of the Lord.'"

This is reiterated by Peter when speaking to the citizens of Jerusalem following the death, resurrection, and ascension of Yeshua to the right hand of the Father.

> Acts 3:19-21 —Therefore repent and return, so that your sins may be wiped away, in order that times of refreshing may come from the presence of the Lord; and that He may send Yeshua, the Messiah appointed for you, who must remain in heaven until the time comes for God to restore everything, which He spoke by the mouth of His holy prophets from ancient time.

Peter exhorts Jewish people to repent of their unbelief in Yeshua not merely that their sins would be forgiven, but that Yeshua will return. For Messiah "must remain in heaven" until Israel nationally accepts Him as their Messiah.

With the Second Coming of the Messiah, Satan will be bound for 1000 years (Revelation 20:1-3). Therefore, Satan is attempting to stop the redemptive program of God. He is trying to destroy the Jewish people through anti-Semitism, and by making faith in Yeshua so abhorrent to any self-respecting Jew, that he would not even consider Yeshua. Praying for Israel's salvation is a vital frontline in the spiritual warfare we are engaged in for Messiah. Since we understand that the return of the Lord is dependent on the repentance of Israel we, like Ruth, will do all we can for Israel's redemptive welfare and their coming to faith in Messiah. Ruth's growing faith is seen in a greater loyalty to Israel's redemptive welfare.

Ruth's Scriptural Decision-Making

Boaz noted that Ruth sought a *goel* and also that she was "not going after young men, whether poor or rich." Ruth sought Boaz, an older man, as a *goel* rather than a younger man.

The phrase "young men" in Hebrew (*bachurim*) refers to desirable, handsome young men. Ruth was making her decision based on faith, not sight which contrary to her generation as seen in Judges 21:25. She sought a redeemer and God's grace (*chesed*). Ruth had demonstrated undivided loyalty to the God of Israel and to Naomi, a quality that is hard to find.

Loyalty means the act of binding yourself (intellectually or emotionally) to a course of action.[5] As one writer, Edwin Hubbel Chapin said, "No more duty can be urged upon those who are entering the great theater of life than simple loyalty to their best convictions."

Loyalty means remaining faithful even when all others are unfaithful. Ruth was loyal to her God and His Word. She is a vivid reminder of a loyalty that Yeshua displayed to His Father. He was faithful to the point of death... even death on the cross. Messiah did not waiver in spite of the sin, wickedness, and betrayal of those for whom he died. Our true hope is founded upon Yeshua's loyalty and faithfulness. The Word of God says, "If we are faithless, He remains faithful, for He cannot deny Himself" (2 Timothy 2:13). Yeshua will never be disloyal or unfaithful to you.

Loyalty is a rare value in most societies. Sculptors in ancient Rome understood the disloyalty of their citizenry, and whenever they would sculpt statue of Rome's heroes, they would sculpt them with detachable heads. Thus, when the current hero fell out of favor, all the sculptor had to do was sculpt another head, rather than an entire statue. Loyalty is not only rare, but also reflective of God's own nature. It is like Yeshua who will never leave us, nor forsake us, because His Word does not change. We, however, by His empowering Holy Spirit and according to His Word, are enabled to be loyal and remain faithful to our Lord and Creator by finishing the course He has laid out for each of us, not quitting, giving up or coasting, but sprinting through the finish line with bold faith.

---

5 Webster's Dictionary

Loyalty has always been a mark of God's presence in our lives, for the Scriptures teach, "A man swears to his own hurt and changes not" (Psalm 15:4).

Your Worries Are Baseless

Ruth 3:11 —Now, my daughter, do not fear. I will do for you whatever you ask, for all my people in the city know that you are a woman of excellence.

Boaz assured Ruth to "fear not" —but what was there to fear? He assured Ruth of his personal involvement to act on her behalf. Previously Ruth had said to Naomi, "All that you say I will do" (Ruth 3:5). Now, Boaz says to Ruth: "All that you say I will do for you." Her words expressed her compliance; his words demonstrated his assurance to her. He would act! Boaz followed a God of truth, so his word is also trustworthy (Psalm 15:4). This is the same confidence we can have in Messiah, our true Redeemer, for He said He will do whatever we ask (John 14:13). All believers in Messiah can, therefore, have a deep and abiding assurance that He is personally at work to accomplish His perfect will for our lives.

Boaz also noted the public acknowledgement of Ruth's valor. Boaz stated why he could freely serve her in this regard, "for all my people in the city know that you are a woman of excellence." Regarding the verse 11 in Ruth chapter three the Targum picks up on the pressure that Ruth would bear in having a godly testimony.

And now, my daughter, do not fear. What you say to me I will do for you, since it is known to all who sit at the gate, the Great Sanhedrin, of my people, that you are a righteous woman and have the strength to bear the yoke of the commandments of the Lord."

Boaz assured her that there would be no shame for him to marry her, despite the fact that Ruth is a Moabite, for her testimony was excellent. This phrase "a woman of excellence" in Hebrew (*eshet-chayil*) implies ability, efficiency, and moral worth. It is used proverbially to describe godly women who are worthy of praise.

Proverbs 12:4 —*An excellent wife* is the crown of her husband.

Proverbs 31:10 —*An excellent wife*, who can find? For her worth is far above gems.

It is interesting to note that in the Septuagint, the Rabbis who translated this word, *chayil* into Greek used the word *dunamos*, which means power. Ruth had a powerful witness in her community.

Messiah also assures us of His enablement, "You will receive power when the Holy Spirit comes upon you, and you will be witnesses of me" (Acts 1:8). Though we may only be gleaners, His testimony is seen as we live for Him.

2 Corinthians 4:7 —But we have this treasure in earthen vessels, that the surpassing greatness of the power may be of God and not from ourselves.

Power is another mark of the believer, "for God has not given us a spirit of timidity, but of power and love and discipline" (2 Timothy 1:7). Boaz was honored to serve someone like Ruth. God loves to bless publicly those that honor Him privately. He can do more for us and with us when we have a godly public testimony (1 Timothy 3:6). We must commit ourselves to live openly and faithfully for the Lord.

ASSURANCE WITHOUT DOUBT

Ruth 3:12-13 —Now it is true I am a close relative [redeemer]; however, there is a relative [redeemer] closer than I. Remain this night, and when morning comes, if he will redeem you, good; let him redeem you. But if he does not wish to redeem you, then I will redeem you, as the LORD lives. Lie down until morning.

Ruth could be confident in Boaz's intentions to redeem her, but she had to be patient for God's timing. Boaz explains what he must do in order to redeem her (thus showing her another aspect of his integrity). If the closer relative will redeem her, then he will submit to the circumstances. If not, then he would certainly be thrilled to redeem her himself. Regardless of the outcome, redemption is assured. When you trust the Lord and obey His Word and leave the results up to God, all things will work together for good. "I will redeem you!" Boaz assured Ruth. In order to give an even deeper assurance to Ruth Boaz added a vow in the Lord, "as the LORD lives." Boaz was saying, "As surely as He lives, you will be redeemed!" In the same way, those who follow God's Word can share the same assurance from the Lord. For we are taught,

Hebrews 6:17-20—In the same way God, desiring even more to show to the heirs of the promise the unchangeableness of His purpose, interposed with an oath, so that by two unchangeable things in which it is impossible for God to lie, we who have taken refuge would have strong encouragement to take hold of the hope set before us. This hope we have as an anchor of the soul, a hope both sure and steadfast and one which enters within the veil, where Yeshua has entered as a forerunner for us, having become a high priest forever.

If Ruth could patiently wait because of Boaz's strong assurance (and she did wait), how can we not have even stronger hope and cause for patience as we wait for Yeshua to complete His work for us and in us? "For I am confident of this very thing, He who began a good work in you will complete it until the day of Messiah Yeshua" (Philippians 1:6). We have faith in a "God who cannot lie" (Titus 1:2). Our patience is because of our confidence in His perfect Word.

ASSURANCE WITHOUT DANGER

Ruth 3:14 —So she lay at his feet until morning and rose before one could recognize another; and he said, "Let it not be known that the woman came to the threshing floor."

Ruth was encouraged, "Lodge here until morning" to protect her reputation from gossip. Ruth's detected presence at the threshing floor could lead to a misinterpretation of her motives. Most likely, Boaz also had a concern for her safety; if she left, she might encounter thieves or men drunk at the harvest season. She slept "at his feet" in humility and purity. She got up before everyone else while it was still dark. Ruth had a good reputation, then why did Boaz caution her in regards to the other sleepers? Her reputation was to be protected on behalf of the other relative (goel), in case he would accept the responsibility. Ruth was to be unblemished from any unwarranted gossip. Likewise, the redeemed are "betrothed to one husband, so that to Messiah I [Paul] might present you as a pure virgin" (2 Corinthians 11:2). Let nothing tarnish our purity in His redemption of us.

The Assuring Works Of Redemption

Boaz's words gave Ruth the assurance of redemption to her, and his works gave the assurance of redemption through her. His works are an assurance of his pledge of sufficiency and his promise of testimony (Ruth 3:15-17).

Ruth 3:15-17 —Again he said, "Give me the cloak that is on you and hold it." So she held it, and he measured six measures of barley and laid it on her. Then she went into the city. 16 When she came to her mother-in-law, she said, "How did it go, my daughter?" And she told her all that the man had done for her. 17 She said, "These six measures of barley he gave to me, for he said, 'Do not go to your mother-in-law empty-handed.'"

What does all this barley have to do with anything? It is Ruth's guarantee. If sent back home empty, it might appear as a disapproval and a rejection of her request for Boaz to be her redeemer. In a sense, it is like a down payment, like a "bride price" so to speak. She was given to carry in her cloak six measures of barley. That is two ephahs, or sixty pounds! That is a lot! Why that much? It was as much as she could bear.

Who is all this abundant blessing for? Ruth? No, Naomi! He gives to Naomi through Ruth. As noted above, we receive abundantly so that we might give graciously to others.

John 7:37-39 —Now on the last day, the great day of the feast, Jesus stood and cried out, saying, "If anyone is thirsty, let him come to Me and drink. "He who believes in Me, as the Scripture said, 'From his innermost being will flow rivers of living water.' " But this He spoke of the

Spirit, whom those who believed in Him were to receive; for the Spirit was not yet given, because Jesus was not yet glorified. "

In our thirst we come to Messiah. Then He fills us so that we might become overflowing streams into the lives of others. We, too, have a down payment of "the first fruits of the Spirit" (Romans 8:23). By the power of this Holy Spirit we are able to minister His living water of love to the thirsting hearts of those around us. Until he returns for us, we have His down payment, a token of all the fullness that is yet to come.

PROMISE OF REDEMPTION

Ruth 3:16-17 —When she came to her mother-in-law, she said, "How did it go, my daughter?" And she told her all that the man had done for her. 17 She said, "These six measures of barley he gave to me, for he said, 'Do not go to your mother-in-law empty-handed.'"

When she arrived back home, Naomi could only ask what she probably had been waiting all night to ask "How did it go, my daughter?" In Hebrew this is literally, "*Mi ott*, or who are you!" This a colloquial way for Naomi to ask: "So now, are you Mrs. Boaz yet?" In a similar way we might also ask: "So, what's the story?" Ruth "declared all that happened." She shared all the wonderful details.

The most exciting news to Naomi was why Boaz gave Ruth six measures of barley. Ruth continued in 3:17, "for he said, 'Do not go to your mother-in-law empty-handed.'" Literally Boaz said, "don't go back empty."

The significance of this is in the word "empty." This is the same word used in Ruth 1:21 ("I went out full, but the LORD has brought me back *empty*") upon Naomi's return to Bethlehem. This word "empty" was how Naomi characterized her life. But now these words from Boaz were ministering directly to her life. Naomi was not "empty" any more! The grain was Naomi's guarantee that her emptiness was over, and like Naomi, the Holy Spirit is our guarantee that we will never be empty again.

The God-shaped void in every heart is what Yeshua fills perfectly with the Holy Spirit. Until the Redeemer returns for us, we, too, have His down payment, a token of all to come. The barley was given as testimony and assurance to Naomi that Ruth was truly redeemed (Ruth 3:17). Though Boaz's words were enough to assure Ruth that she would certainly be redeemed, his gift was to assure Naomi of the same fact. In these gracious works of Boaz through Ruth to Naomi we can see a picture of the purpose of good works in our lives: to verify the Redeemer's redemption of us; it is His proof through us that we are His and that His Word is true. The Scriptures tell us that our works testify to others that we are truly saved. "I will show you my faith by my works" (James 2:18). The Scriptures assure us that these good works have always been the plan of God's assurance through us.

Ephesians 2:10 —For we are His workmanship, created in Messiah Yeshua for good works, which God prepared beforehand so that we would walk in them.

These works are our loving testimony that we are truly His, for Yeshua said, "By this all men will know you are my disciples if you love one another" (John 13:34-35).

Good works and all fruit bearing is merely the evidence of our abiding in Him; it's His testimony through us of our redemption. The power of good works is illustrated in an old rabbinical story:

> When Joseph was Prime Minister to Pharaoh during the period of the famine, he emptied the chaff of his granaries into the river Nile. It floated far away, and the people at a great distance below saw it. The chaff indicated that there was plenty of grain up the river, which gave hope that there was food during the famine.

Our works may be seen only as chaff, but they are proof of His great redemption and provision for all who will believe. The assurance of waiting for redemption ministered through Naomi to Ruth.

Ruth was assured by Naomi to wait when she said: "Wait, my daughter, until you know how the matter turns out; for the man will not rest until he has settled it today" (Ruth 3:18). Ruth did her part by faith. We are told that by faith "those that wait upon the Lord will renew their strength, they will mount with wings like eagles" (Isaiah 40: 31). Nonetheless, faith that waits upon the Lord can often be a struggle.

How To Wait By Faith

Ruth 3:18 —Then she said, "Wait, my daughter, until you know how the matter turns out; for the man will not rest until he has settled it today."

Naomi said to her, "Wait, my daughter." The ability to wait can be difficult. However, waiting shows trust in the *goel's* work until all is completed by Him.

As in Lamentations 3:26 says, "It is good that he waits silently for the salvation of the LORD." When we wait on the Lord we display our complete trust in Him.

Romans 8:23 —We having the first fruits of the Spirit, *waiting* eagerly for our adoption as sons, the redemption of our body.

Galatians 5:5 —For we through the Spirit, by faith, are *waiting* for the hope of righteousness.

James 5:7 —Therefore be patient, brethren, until the coming of the Lord. The farmer waits for the precious produce of the soil, *being patient* about it, until it gets the early and late rains.

Naomi continued, "until you know how the matter turns out." Literally it states: "sit (*yashav!*) until you know." Faith acts on facts. Sometime acting on what we believe means waiting until we have somewhere to go. God is in control. It is best to wait on Him. In His perfect timing He will reveal to us His will and plan, but we must learn how to wait on Him. God will always do exactly as He has promised. He is never early. He will never be late.

When I first went to share Messiah in the Ukraine, it was still under the Soviet socialist system. The hotel room I was given had a window curtain that only covered half of the window. I complained to the person at the desk that the curtain did not cover the window. She said, "Yes, aren't we smart. We took a curtain for one window and cut it half to use for two rooms!" I was astonished and said, "But with this kind of service, no one will want to return to this hotel!" The reply from the desk was, "Return? We never expect anyone to return!"

Their service lived out their conviction that they really never expected anyone to return. Are we acting in such a way that it looks like we do not expect Messiah, our Redeemer, to return?

Waiting on the Lord can be hard for most of us. It is during the period of waiting when we can be tempted to sin. It was when Moses was delayed on Mount Sinai that the Israelites became "antsy" —made the golden calf and sinned (Exodus 32:1-6). Messiah warned us in Matthew 25:5, "Now while the bridegroom was delaying, they all got drowsy and began to sleep." Let us not grow weary in well doing! His Word gives assurance to our souls, and His resulting works through us will testify to all who see that we are redeemed!

Naomi concludes her wise counsel to Ruth, "for the man will not rest until he has finished it today." The Hebrew word *kalah* means to bring to an end, to complete, or to finish. In other words Naomi was assuring Ruth that her *goel* will be working on her behalf to accomplish the matter that was begun. For us as well, we can be confident that "He who began a good work in you will perfect it until the day of Messiah Yeshua" (Philippians 1:6).

CHAPTER 12

REDEMPTION BY LOVE

THE PROPOSAL OF THE LAW OF LOVE

Ruth 4:1-12 —Now Boaz went up to the gate and sat down there, and behold, the close relative of whom Boaz spoke was passing by, so he said, "Turn aside, friend, sit down here." And he turned aside and sat down. 2 He took ten men of the elders of the city and said, "Sit down here." So they sat down. 3 Then he said to the closest relative, "Naomi, who has come back from the land of Moab, has to sell the piece of land which belonged to our brother Elimelech. 4 "So I thought to inform you, saying, 'Buy it before those who are sitting here, and before the elders of my people. If you will redeem it, redeem it; but if not, tell me that I may know; for there is no one but you to redeem it, and I am after you.' " And he said, "I will redeem it." 5 Then Boaz said, "On the day you buy the field from the hand of Naomi, you must also acquire Ruth the Moabitess, the widow of the deceased, in order to raise up the name of the deceased on his inheritance." 6 The closest relative said, "I cannot redeem it for myself, because I would jeopardize my own inheritance. Redeem it for yourself; you may have my right of redemption, for I cannot redeem it." 7 Now this was the custom in former times in Israel concerning the redemption and the exchange of land to confirm any matter: a man removed his sandal and gave it to another; and this was the manner of attestation in Israel. 8 So the closest relative said to Boaz, "Buy it for yourself." And he removed his sandal. 9 Then Boaz said to the elders and all the people, "You are witnesses today that I have bought from the hand of Naomi all that belonged to Elimelech and all that belonged to Chilion and Mahlon. 10 "Moreover, I have acquired Ruth the Moabitess, the widow of Mahlon, to be my wife in order to raise up the name of the deceased on his inheritance, so that the name of the deceased will not be cut off from his brothers or from the court of his birth place; you are witnesses today." 11 All the people who were in the court, and the elders, said, "We are witnesses. May the LORD make the woman who is coming into your home like Rachel and Leah, both of whom built the house of Israel; and may you achieve wealth in Ephrathah and become famous in Bethlehem. 12 "Moreover, may your house be like the house of Perez whom Tamar bore to Judah, through the offspring which the LORD will give you by this young woman."

It is not always easy to set proper priorities on some tough calls. There is a humorous story that illustrates this: A group of friends who went deer hunting separated into pairs for the day. That night, one hunter returned alone, staggering under an eight-point buck. The other hunters asked, "Where's Harry?" The man told him, "Harry fainted a couple miles up the trail." The others couldn't believe it. "You mean you left him lying there alone and carried the deer back?" The man answered, "It was a tough call, but I figured no one is going to steal Harry."

This portion of Ruth 4:1-12 will help us develop eternal values that can properly evaluate our priorities and show us what is worthy of our time, talent, and treasure. In this section, we will consider:

- The priority for redemption -Ruth 4:1-5
- The purpose of redemption -Ruth 4:6-10
- The power in redemption -Ruth 4:11-12

The issue of redemption is always God's main concern. Boaz lived up to God's priorities as a kinsman-redeemer. He was ready, willing and able to redeem. Boaz's work for Ruth's redemption is seen as his highest priority by his initiative, diligence, and patience. He brought all his authority to bear. There was nothing else of greater importance to Boaz and God.

Even though it was harvest time, the busiest and most lucrative time of the year, Boaz dropped everything to be an instrument of redemption. The harvest of grain was secondary to a harvest of souls. He put the redemption of Ruth the Moabitess above his own business.

Ruth 4:1—Now Boaz went up to the gate and sat down there, and behold, the close relative of whom Boaz spoke was passing by, so he said, "Turn aside, friend, sit down here." And he turned aside and sat down. 2 He took tenmen of the elders of the city and said, "Sit down here." So they sat down.

Boaz went to "the gate" of Bethlehem, because it was the place of business and judgment for the city.[6]

6 Normally, elders would be gathered there to provide counsel for the community. If elders were not at the gate for settling disputes, this was a sign that a catastrophe had occurred in the community as described in Lamentations 5:14.

Boaz had acted faithfully and now he waited on the Lord to bring the plan of redemption together. Boaz did not have to wait too long for the text states, "Behold!" In Hebrew the word "behold" is *hine* and it has an implication of getting the attention of the listener, as if to exclaim: "God is at work!"

When the closer relative passes by Boaz tells him to turn aside. Boaz does more than encourage him to sit down. The phrase "turn aside" is one word in Hebrew, *sur,*[7] and it is in the imperative, which implies that the person must listen. One can almost sense a plea from Boaz that this other man *turn aside* from his own priorities and put God's business first. In Ruth 4:2 Boaz says, "Turn aside, *friend*, sit down here." The Hebrew word for friend is *peloni almoni* and literally means a certain someone or a certain so and so. In all likelihood, he was a well-known person in the community, however, his name is not mentioned to graciously keep him from shame. Further in this chapter we will call the closer relative, Peloni, as he is also known traditionally.

According to the law of levirate marriage from Deuteronomy 25, the widow needed to initiate a process of redemption and was to approach the kinsman, and then the elders. Boaz probably knew this man well enough to know that he would turn Ruth down. And rather than have Ruth face the public rejection, Boaz interceded on Ruth's behalf. Boaz used his influence and authority to gather "the witnesses" (Ruth 4:9).

---

7 This same word used in Exodus 3:3-4 and Numbers 12:10. The root of *sur* is often used of Israel's apostasy. In the *Theological Wordbook* of the Old Testament, the root of the word *sur* is used repeatedly of Israel and its leaders that they "*did not depart* from the sins of Jeroboam" (2 Kings 10:31). In many cases it is translated, "turn aside or away" (Exodus 32:8; Deuteronomy 9:12; 11:16).

He told the elders to "sit here" in command form. "And they sat." It certainly seems that Boaz was a man of authority, for they did it without a question. He rounded up ten[8] elders, though two witnesses would have been enough for an ordinary case, even a murder trial (Deuteronomy 17:6). Boaz took this transaction very seriously. He wanted to make sure that everything was done properly, since Ruth was a Moabite woman and it could become a sticking point in the transaction.

In principle, the righteous desire a public witness, whereas sinners love the dark. Our redemption is made public by God in Romans 3:24-26,

> Being justified as a gift by His grace through the redemption which is in Messiah Yeshua; whom God displayed publicly as an atoning sacrifice in His blood through faith. This was to demonstrate His righteousness, because in the forbearance of God He passed over the sins previously committed; for the demonstration, I say, of His righteousness at the present time, so that He would be just and the justifier of the one who has faith in Yeshua.

Through Messiah's death on the cross God publicly redeemed us, and He is unashamed to declare us to the heavenly host as His brethren (Matthew 10:32-33; Hebrews 2:11). Likewise we are to be unashamed of the Good News, and confess Yeshua publicly.

Boaz used all that he had in his possession: initiative, diligence, patience, authority, and influence. Why? Because everything God gives us is to be used for His redemptive purposes.

---

8 There are various theories about the reason for the "ten" elders (i.e., minyan/quorum) for public assembly, or for holding a wedding, or some think to represent the ten commandments, which represents the whole Torah, which would witness to the event.

Indeed, we are to "redeem the time, for the days are evil" (Ephesians 5:16). As Yeshua our Redeemer came "to seek and to save that which is lost" (Luke 19:10), so Boaz put redemption of others above his own business. How much of your time, talent, and treasure is dedicated for redemption? One day we will all be brought before the Lord to be evaluated on how we used what we had and whether it was used for His purposes or to fulfill the desires of our flesh.

REDEMPTION PRESENTATION

Ruth 4:3-5—Then he said to the closest relative, "Naomi, who has come back from the land of Moab, has to sell the piece of land which belonged to our brother Elimelech. 4 "So I thought to inform you, saying, 'Buy before those who are sitting, and before the elders of my people. If you will redeem, redeem ; but if not, tell me that I may know; for there is no one but you to redeem, and I am after you.'" And he said, "I will redeem."

Rather than bringing up the matter of Ruth, Boaz brought up the matter of family property first. It was a redemptive matter to keep the land in the family. Boaz referred to Naomi's deceased husband Elimelech, as "our brother." He may have been speaking generally about a family member, or Elimelech may have been his brother as well as the brother of the unnamed "nearer" kinsman who traditionally is known as Peloni. That would make Boaz the younger brother and Peloni the older brother, who would naturally have had first right of redemption. Though Boaz had a greater desire for the opportunity, Peloni had a greater right. Boaz trusted the Lord by handling it properly, in all fairness and righteousness.

Boaz handled it personally: the text translates the Hebrew as "so I thought to inform you." Literally it means, "so I said I'd uncover you ear," that is, I would lift the turban fold to speak personally to the person. This conveys a bit more intimacy. Clearly, Boaz was handling this personally and not through an intermediary.

Boaz handled it publicly: Boaz took the matter to the elders. Nothing was done in secret. There were no hidden agendas and no money was traded under the table. There were witnesses, which proved to be a clear testimony of righteousness.

Boaz handled it plainly: Boaz stated, "If you'll redeem it, redeem! If not, declare to me! I will know." Nothing is uncertain; it is a clear, straightforward transaction on the land. The reason for this is that it carries the implication: "if you don't redeem it, I will."

This reminds me somewhat of a certain situation when I was single. I was quite smitten and attracted to Miriam. I thought my friend was dating her. So I asked him, "What are your intentions toward Miriam?" He looked confused. He had no intentions of marrying her. So he responded, "Huh?" Undaunted I continued, "Because if you don't marry her, I will!" To this, his eyes grew wide as saucers, and he said, "Huh?" With that, I went ahead and asked Miriam out on a date. So with the issue of the land clearly presented to Peloni, he responded to Boaz saying, "I myself will redeem."

Does Boaz's approach reflect your own dealings? Boaz's approach to redeem demonstrates his integrity: he was personally direct, publicly open, and painfully clear.

In the same way God is clear on all His promises to us that we might have confidence in His Word for our lives. But there is still one more issue to be resolved: Ruth.

> Ruth 4:5 —Then Boaz said, "On the day you buy the field from the hand of Naomi, you must also acquire Ruth the Moabitess, the widow of the deceased, in order to raise up the name of the deceased on his inheritance."

Once Peloni agreed to redeem the land, Boaz informed him that "to get the land you must take Ruth to *raise up* the name of the deceased." The word that Boaz used, "to raise up (or establish) the name of the deceased" is the same word and form which is used in the laws for a levirate marriage stated in Deuteronomy 25:7, "to establish a name for his brother in Israel." Boaz was clearly letting Peloni know that the matter was not only to be the redeemer of the land, but also of his brother's name through levirate marriage to Ruth.

Why did Boaz do it this way? Why did he apparently "spring" this on Peloni only after Peloni said yes to the land? Boaz wanted the issue to be about the essence of God's Word, the priority of people over possessions. If Boaz had put both the land and Ruth in the same offer and he turned it down, we would not know whether he turned down the land or Ruth. Boaz states, "to raise up the name of the deceased on his inheritance," that is, the land will still be Mahlon's inheritance through the seed with Ruth. It would never permanently be Peloni's land while Ruth was in the picture. The land would always be there to bless the family of Elimelech through Mahlon through the seed of Ruth. The land was to bless the seed, not Peloni.

Similarly there are "Pelonis" in this world to this day. Welfare scam artists that attempt to get money for foster children with no children ever being helped. You should only get the money if you actually care for the people; the money is for the children's welfare not to line your pockets. King Solomon cared about the people, therefore he asked God for wisdom to minister to them well, and did not ask for wealth and fame (1 Kings 3:5-13). Nevertheless, God gave Solomon wealth and fame, for God knew that Solomon's priorities reflected His priorities: helping people. The redeemed ones use their resources to redeem people; the unredeemed use people to get things. For Boaz, Ruth was actually the main purpose of the transaction; the land was a secondary matter. But to Peloni, the issue was only the land, not the person. The way Boaz handled the situation revealed that the priority of God's Word was redemption of people first, then the blessings of the land. When we care about people, then the blessings follow, because the blessings are given so we could care for people.

THE PURPOSE OF REDEMPTION IS FOR ALL PEOPLE

Ruth 4:6-8 —The closest relative said, "I cannot redeem for myself, because I would jeopardize my own inheritance. Redeem it for yourself; you may have my right of redemption, for I cannot redeem it." 7 Now this was the custom in former times in Israel concerning the redemption and the exchange of land to confirm any matter: a man removed his sandal and gave it to another; and this was the manner of attestation in Israel. 8 So the closest relative said to Boaz, "Buy it for yourself." And he removed his sandal.

When faced with the need to include Ruth in his life, Peloni responds, "I cannot redeem," or more literally, "I am not able." He was powerless. How can that be, since he was called to be a redeemer? Are you unable to do what God has called you to do as dad, mom, or friend? Why are people so unable to do what God created and called them to do? It is sort of like duct tape. There are many uses for duct tape: tape up a bicycle seat, seal a leaky radiator hose, secure a broken window, or keep an alligator's mouth shut. But amazingly, you cannot depend on duct tape to fulfill its primary purpose: sealing heating/air-conditioning ducts. Max Sherman, a physicist who conducted experiments to monitor the effectiveness of various air-conditioning and heating sealants concluded that duct tape almost always failed and resulted in approximately 30% loss of the heat and cool air generated in the average home.

Like duct tape, we may be failing at the primary purpose for which we were created. God created us for His pleasure: to bring honor and glory to His Name. He created us in His image to relate to Him that we might then represent Him. But He also created us to depend on Him in order to function properly. Life was never meant to be lived apart from Him. He always calls us to live a life beyond our own power so that we will depend on His grace by faith in Messiah. In Messiah we can do everything God called us to do, but apart from Him we can do nothing that He created us to do (Philippians 4:13; John 15:5).

Psalm 18:29 —For by You I can run upon a troop; and by my God I can leap over a wall.

Selfishness Was Peloni's motivation

Peloni gives the reason why he could not redeem Ruth "for myself." In Hebrew, Peloni said literally, "to me" (*lee*) or "on my behalf." Peloni showed no concern for the name of his brother, but only for how it would further his own self interests. If you want to be a spiritual failure, be self-centered in all you do. When you do not live in a God-centered universe, then you have a self-centered system. Peloni's selfishness is the cause of his faithlessness. Redemption is not a selfish, but rather a selfless activity.

Greediness Was Peloni's Goal

When Peloni stated, "because I would jeopardize my own inheritance." He revealed his concern that his own inheritance would be jeopardized, that is, literally, destroyed or ruined (*shachath*). I'll be ruined! Maintaining his own possessions meant more to him than maintaining his brother's name. He could be concerned that Ruth's child would get the property and could make a claim on his property. If he had no other children but the one by Ruth, then that child would have Peloni's land and Peloni's own name would not be carried on. And if he had other children, it might bring a legal concern for their inheritance. The problem of levirate marriage is that it confused the lines of inheritance even inside the land.

Ruth is a Moabite —a ruined foreigner, and a poor gleaner. It would ruin his own inheritance, indeed. There may have been real question in his mind whether a Moabite could make a legal claim in Israel (Deuteronomy 23:3-6); it might all be lost. Of course, there might have been a bit of prejudice involved with this concern as well. There may have been social and, legal or economic repercussions to being married to a Moabite. Just being an Israeli patriot might have been enough to reject a Moabite from consideration. "Sure," he may have thought, "Mahlon's name is maintained, but now my name is messed up!" His inability to accept graciously someone different than himself would suggest a man who was not depending on grace for his own walk with God.

When Naomi in her poverty had to sell her field, the next-of-kin was obligated to buy it back for her. This Peloni was willing to do for his brother's widow without issue. When he learned that he had to marry Ruth and raise children who would maintain Mahlon's inheritance, he refused; he wanted the land, but not if it included Ruth. The land was an additional advantage; Peloni saw Ruth as a disadvantage.

Here is where faith comes into play on these matters: if you will faithfully be your brother's keeper then God will be your keeper. Each of us has to make a faith-decision when it comes to being a follower of the Lord. Will it be God's will or our own? Peloni might have thought, "I cannot fulfill my agenda by God's will! In fact, following God is not in my own best interests." Without faith in God, he missed the real point of life: God's will is your best interest. As Matthew instructs, "seek first the kingdom of God and His righteousness and all these other things will be added unto you!" The point of our lives is supposed to be concern for our brothers. The law of love and being our brother's keeper is in our own best interests.

There can be no lasting honor when a life is oriented around self and not sacrifice for others. Redemption always involves cost and a sacrifice. As a deliverer, there are captors to be overcome. If a blood avenger, there is a murderer to subdue. If there is land redemption, there is wealth to be available. If there is a brother's name to be maintained for Israel to continue, there has to be a willingness to sacrifice. Essentially, Ruth was not the real problem; it was the sacrifice to be the redeemer that was the problem. David would not offer to God what did not cost him (2 Samuel 24:24). Peloni was not willing to pay the price.

Are you willing to sacrifice in order to redeem? Peloni serves as a reminder that even the best-known of people cannot redeem us. Peloni's problem is not the land, he agreed to that; his problem was greedy self-interest. Yeshua the Redeemer gave all in order to fully redeem us. Those that follow Him demonstrate that a true redeemer prioritizes people over possessions. Redeemers use possessions to secure people, and never use people to secure possessions. Peloni certainly was a man of his age. As the book of Judges describes, "In those days there was no king in Israel; everyone did what was right in his own eyes." He cared little for how it appeared in the eyes of the Lord. How it seemed in his own eyes was how he lived, and it revealed the awful truth that he was not living for the Lord.

Do you seek more money for more things or to help people? Do you follow the Redeemer of grace or Peloni of greed?

Shamelessness Was Peloni's Forte

In Ruth 4:7-8, the writer reminds the readers regarding the public shame that accompanied one who would not fulfill the duty to carry on his brother's name through levirate marriage. So with Peloni's words, "Buy it for yourself," he followed the custom of removing his sandal, which is the same word that is used in Deuteronomy 25:10. The text states, "this was the custom," and it became, as it states in Deuteronomy, "a testimony in Israel."

The removal of the shoe served two redemptive functions in light of Deuteronomy 25:10 and Leviticus 25:25, in regards to the land issue. In accordance with Deuteronomy 25:9-10, the removal of his shoe was a symbolic statement that Peloni forsook his right to plant his foot on the property to control the land and the lady. It was still too early in Israel's history for these matters to be dealt in writing by lawyers (as in Jeremiah 32:10). It was considered a valid transaction if conducted in the presence of valid witnesses.

The shoe, like a contract, was a binding symbol of the actual transaction and the transfer of rights. If the owner would not surrender the land, the shoe would be the contract, the proof of a valid transaction. It was a disgrace in Israel to be unwilling to redeem a relative. Walking barefoot testifies publicly of this disgrace. I can imagine how this might have struck Peloni: "Er, Boaz... I didn't come with an extra sandal!" Selfishness and greed are so strong that many will surrender their own dignity, integrity, and self respect to gain possessions, prestige, or power. Peloni was like the people on some TV shows who are willing to degrade themselves for their fifteen minutes of fame. Sin shames you now and forever. As noted, the name Peloni is traditional; it was not recorded in Scripture. He who would not preserve his brother's name does not preserve his own name either. He rejected the calling, and therefore lost the honor as well. God's will for you is discernable, but if you say, "No, it'll interfere with my own agenda!" you will not hear: "well-done, good and faithful servant." Your name, like the nameless nearer kinsman in Ruth will be "least in the kingdom of heaven" (Matthew 5:19).

Peloni did not care, do you? His shamelessness was his undoing and led to his eternal shamefulness. The true irony of the matter is that through Ruth, God established the line of Messiah (Matthew 1:5). The honor to be a part of that line that was offered to Peloni went to Boaz. What Peloni thought would ruin his portfolio would have been the key to his eternal redemption. What he thought would ruin his reputation would have inscribed him in the Scriptures forever as a hero of the faith. The world has not yet seen what Messiah can do with someone who is fully set apart unto God – by faith in Messiah you can be that person.

Redemption Has A Selfless Purpose

Ruth 4:9-10 —Then Boaz said to the elders and all the people, "You are witnesses today that I have bought from the hand of Naomi all that belonged to Elimelech and all that belonged to Chilion and Mahlon. 10 Moreover, I have acquired Ruth the Moabitess, the widow of Mahlon, to be my wife in order to raise up the name of the deceased on his inheritance, so that the name of the deceased will not be cut off from his brothers or from the court of his place; you are witnesses today."

Redemption was costly for Boaz. In stating twice "all that belonged" to the departed, not only did Boaz assume oversight of the land, but he also accepted the fact that all her debts were his, too. Anyone with a grievance against Naomi now had to go to Boaz. His wealth was at stake for the purpose of redemption. In the same way our Messiah "though rich, He made Himself poor that we might be rich in Him" (2 Corinthians 8:9).

In fact, Yeshua "who knew no sin became sin (offering) on our behalf that we might become the righteousness of God in Him" (2 Corinthians 5:21). He gave up His own life for our redemption. And now our sin debts are covered by His righteousness. His grace is our sufficiency. Any charge from Satan against you must be brought to Him. Presently interceding on our behalf, He says, "I have that covered!" Therefore we can rest secure in Him forever.

Boaz's Declaration Of The Redemption

Boaz declared, "Ruth is to be my wife in order to raise up the name of the deceased, her dead husband, Mahlon." Please note that Boaz was motivated by the law of love – it was the deceased name that was his concern. His essential purpose was to obey God's Word to maintain Israel (Deuteronomy 25:6). Boaz declared, "I am my brother's keeper, Israel's sustainer and God's servant."

Wisdom recognizes that the purpose driven life is for the purpose of redemption. The Scripture gives each of us an eternal purpose for our daily lives at our job, marriage, and friendships. God's essential purpose for your life is to care about the eternal welfare of people –those around you, and those around the world.

As we identify with God in Messiah, His love will be seen in our lives through our priorities and decisions – whether at work or on vacation.

The purpose of the land redemption in this book was to acquire the person's redemption. Messiah taught us a parable that referred to this very matter. He said, "The kingdom of heaven is like a treasure hidden in the field, which a man found and hid again; and from joy over it he goes and sells all that he has and buys that field" (Matthew 13:44). The hidden treasure is His people, and so He acquires the field in order to acquire the people. As Messiah taught, so Boaz did. He acquired the field to redeem Ruth.

The pop singer Madonna gained early notoriety by stating as her life purpose, "I want to rule the world." Many might feel the same way, although in all modesty they might be satisfied with a bit less and say, "I want Hawaii" or "I'll take Paris!" God might give you some area but, as Peloni found out, with the land come the people too. Will you love the people there? God would give you the great blessings if you will care for the people with them. But be careful, you might get a "Moabitess" even as Boaz publicly recognized Ruth's heritage (Ruth 4:5,10).

Since Moabites were *persona non grata* as noted in Torah, why would Boaz bring up such a politically incorrect issue? Why did he bring up her weakest area? He mentioned the 'weakness' of her nationality because in her weakness was strength in God's grace. Boaz's comment reminds us that if you cannot love someone at their weakest point, you do not love them at all. If you cannot accept people for who they are, you do not really accept them; you are only accepting an idealized image of the person. But our true Redeemer accepts us just as we are.

Salvation is a 'come as you are' party, because everyone is a "Moabite" spiritually. Our sins have alienated us from God as revealed by the Torah. But the Redeemer accepts us and saves us fully by grace through faith in Yeshua (Ephesians 2:8-9).

Peloni's identity is lost in oblivion because of his rejection of redemption. But those who love as Messiah loves will be honored with Messiah. Boaz looked with compassion upon the needy widows and therefore, Boaz is honored forever in Him. As Moses, who was willing to identify with God's people, so also all who are involved in God's redemptive work are a picture of the true Redeemer. Yeshua looked with compassion upon a lost humanity for they were as sheep without a shepherd (Matthew 9:36). He gave His all as our Redeemer in order to save us forever. As Boaz declared not only to the elders, but to "all the people" there, so Yeshua is not ashamed of us and declares us before the entire heavenly host (Matthew 10:32). We are completely accepted in the Beloved.

If only we could see life from eternity's point of view, we would give all for redemption. But one has assured us of eternity's point of view – Yeshua! He was raised from the dead and He commissioned us to make disciples of all nations, to seek first the kingdom of God, and to live our lives for God. Paul clearly understood that with his afflictions, the investment of his own time, talent, and treasure was the best investment for his life:

2 Corinthians 4:17 —For momentary, light affliction is producing for us an eternal weight of glory far beyond all comparison.

1 Corinthians 2:9 —Eye has not seen, nor has ear heard, nor has it entered into the mind of man what God has prepared for those that love Him.

I believe that the greatest reward for our service of obedience to Messiah will be to hear Him say, "Well done good and faithful servant." Yeshua related to us, the people in need. Through the incarnation, Messiah took on the frailty of our flesh. In order for us to trust and obey Him, He showed us what obedience entailed.

Hebrews 2:14 —Therefore, since the children share in flesh and blood, He Himself likewise also partook of the same.

He loved us enough to endure the pain and the shame of the cross, that we would not have eternal shame. Therefore, let all eternal praise and everlasting glory be given to that Name which above every name, even Yeshua the Messiah.

THE POWER OF REDEMPTION

Ruth 4:11-12 –Then the elders and all those at the gate said, "We are witnesses. May the LORD make the woman who is coming into your home like Rachel and Leah, who together built up the house of Israel. May you have standing in Ephrathah and be famous in Bethlehem. 12Through the offspring the LORD gives you by this young woman, may your family be like that of Perez, whom Tamar bore to Judah."

Now comes a tense moment for Boaz and Ruth. How would the community respond to this redemption and declaration by Boaz? The couple received the blessing of the people.

Those that follow God's will are promised blessing, because faithfulness brings fulfillment. The blessings reflect the obvious faithfulness of Boaz and Ruth as well understanding God's call upon them (Ruth 4:11-12).

The people now recognized that they "were witnesses" —but not merely witnesses of some legal transaction, but witnesses of the work of grace before their eyes. Though Peloni was now walking home like a defeated 'shoeless Joe Jackson,' the people responded as if the occasion had become a wedding celebration for Boaz and Ruth.

All those who attend a wedding are there to witness to the work of God in the lives of the couple. There is a twofold witness involved at all weddings: a witness to the vows that are made by the couple and also to the blessing of God upon the couple. The guests also have a responsibility because of this twofold witness. They get to remind the couple, "What do you mean divorce? I was there when you vowed in the name of the Lord that it was 'until death do us part.'" When difficult trials come upon the couple these same witnesses can remind them of God's blessings, which are based upon His gracious and powerful promises for all of God's people in general and for their marriage in particular. And so the witnesses at this redemption of Ruth by Boaz blessed the couple, desiring only the best of God's goodness for their family.

Therefore, they blessed Ruth: "May the Lord make her like Rachel and Leah." As Rachel and Leah had to leave their families to follow God (Genesis 31:55), so also Ruth. As Ruth (a Moabite) was rejected by Peloni, so Leah was not loved by her husband. Like Ruth, Rachel was initially unable to have children.

God will enable Ruth to do what is needed in order to establish a house. The Hebrew makes it quite clear. It is by God's doing that Ruth came into Boaz' house to establish it like the house of Israel.

Psalm 127:1 —Unless the Lord builds the house, they labor in vain who build it.

The blessing embraces the idea, "May your home be an extension of the House of Israel!" Why did Ruth enter Boaz' house? She entered to build it like the House of Israel was built. Think about your own home and family. When the Lord is the builder of your home and His grace is your sufficiency then your household will bring glory to His Name and serve as a testimony to those around you.

When the people at the gate additionally blessed, "And may you achieve wealth in Ephrathah and become famous in Bethlehem," they were saying, "May her coming into your house bring excellence into Ephrathah, and reputation into Bethlehem!" This is the result of the Lord's building the house. The word for "wealth" in Hebrew is *chayil*. Although *chayil* can be translated as wealth meaning power or might, it is used elsewhere in Ruth to describe worthiness (Ruth 2:1, 3:11). *Chayil* is understood as virtuous valor, since Ruth was quite poor, it is more like speaking of excellence of character that will bring about a great reputation for the community.

Virtue precedes reputation. Do you want a great reputation? Great faith that leads to great faithfulness is what leads to great honor. Do not pray to be merely harmless, but to be helpful. Be proactive in caring for those around you.

Notice carefully the blessing: "May the Lord." Some might foolishly think, "Why bring God into the picture? After all, Boaz and Ruth make a great couple – two *chayil* believers getting married –they have it made in the shade!" True, both are great believers, but that is not enough. We need the Lord, not just a functional spouse! Trust in the Lord for the right person, and then trust in the Lord for a right relationship with that person. Continually seek His grace, which alone is what *chayil* believers depend upon for a victorious life.

HIS PROMISED MINISTRY TO OBEDIENT FAILURES

Ruth 4:12 —Moreover, may your house be like the house of Perez whom Tamar bore to Judah, through the offspring which the LORD will give you by this young woman.

The blessings continued from the witnesses, but now the people were hoping that the couple's children would be "like Perez, who Tamar bore to Judah." This is referring to Israel's history hundreds of years earlier (Genesis 38). God used a levirate marriage with Tamar to maintain the house of Judah through Perez. If God could use a levirate marriage then, He could use this one as well. Perez was one of five families that made up Judah; and a progenitor of Bethlehem's citizens. Boaz was descended from Perez. Perez's parents' levirate marriage in the past was the foundation of Boaz's and Ruth's.

We also read in Ruth 4:20-21 that Boaz was from Salmon, who was married to Rahab, a Canaanite. Rahab, like Ruth, had heard the report of God and believed.

By the same faith they both were grafted into the family Olive Tree. A Canaanite or a Moabite – God uses the weak things of this world to show the sufficiency of His grace. His promises to bless are based on His power to fulfill!

Romans 1:16 says, "The Good News is the power of God for salvation!" It is His redemptive power that brings you into relationship with Him so that you might then minister His redemptive grace to others.

On March 15, 2004, five believers in Messiah were traveling by car to conduct relief efforts in Mosul, Iraq. Without warning, the vehicle was assaulted by automatic weapon fire and rocket-propelled grenades. The car was torn apart, and three of the workers were killed at the scene. Amazingly, David McDonnall, despite being mortally wounded, pulled his wife Niki from the wreckage. She had been shot at least twenty times, but still was alive. Desperate to save her life, David got Niki to a hospital where she was rushed into surgery. When Niki awakened about a week later, she learned that her husband had not survive. His last effort was to save her life. The purpose of Nicki's husband's life was fulfilled. It was not to secure his own life, but the life of another.

Redeemers know that there is fulfillment in redemption, so they give their lives today for the salvation of others. Yeshua said in Luke 9:24, "For whoever wishes to save his life will lose it, but whoever loses his life for My sake, he is the one who will save it."

Peloni never understood that redeemers never use people to secure possessions, but they use possessions and even their lives to secure people.

CHAPTER 13

GOD'S REDEMPTION

HIS COMPLETION OF YOUR RESTORATION

Ruth 4:13-22 — So Boaz took Ruth, and she became his wife, and he went in to her. And the LORD enabled her to conceive, and she gave birth to a son. 14 Then the women said to Naomi, "Blessed is the LORD who has not left you without a redeemer today, and may his name become famous in Israel. 15 "May he also be to you a restorer of life and a sustainer of your old age; for your daughter-in-law, who loves you and is better to you than seven sons, has given birth to him." 16 Then Naomi took the child and laid him in her lap, and became his nurse. The neighbor women gave him a name, saying, "A son has been born to Naomi!" 17 So they named him Obed. He is the father of Jesse, the father of David. 18 Now these are the generations of Perez: to Perez was born Hezron, 19 and to Hezron was born Ram, and to Ram, Amminadab, 20 and to Amminadab was born Nahshon, and to Nahshon, Salmon, 21 and to Salmon was born Boaz, and to Boaz, Obed, 22 and to Obed was born Jesse, and to Jesse, David.

Boaz wins the right to redeem the land and to marry Ruth. Mission accomplished! Not quite. That was not the goal. The goal was not just to marry Ruth. In the beginning of the book of Ruth, Naomi left Israel for Moab during a famine. Naomi was living self-centeredly and apart from God with little concern for Israel. Boaz's main goal of redemption was not only to bring Ruth and Naomi rest for their souls, but also to restore them back to the Lord and to service for His people.

The restoration of Naomi was not merely that she was back in the land, but also returned to fellowship with the Lord. How did this actually take place for Naomi, and how does it take place for the rest of us? Part of the answer was through Obed, the child of Boaz and Ruth. Obed was really a child of grace in his miracle birth (4:13); in his miracle life (4:14-16); and finally in his miracle lineage (4:17-22). In this last section we see that because of God's ability (4:13), loyalty (4:14-16), and sovereignty (4:17-22) ordinary believers like you and me can have eternally-fulfilling lives.

The text says, "So Boaz took Ruth, and she became his wife." Ruth was accepted by the city and was greatly blessed. The marriage was a blessing for the whole community. Early on in this book, Orpah[1] went back to her own people and is never to be heard of again. Orpah, like Peloni, made her choice apart from God's Word and is now lost in obscurity. In contrast to Orpah, Ruth displayed faith and trust in the Lord and did not forsake the Jewish people.

---

1 Jewish tradition holds that Orpah was the ancestor to Goliath; you can picture the confrontation between David and Goliath as being a confrontation between what David and Goliath respectively represented.

Ruth forsook all she had for God and His people, and was blessed for eternity. She married Boaz. Now she was the lady of the farm over the same workers who had to be warned to not be unkind to her. God blesses and brings Boaz and Ruth together to prove that His grace is sufficient. If it is not a miracle of grace that gets you married; it is certainly the miracle of grace that keeps you married! God's blessing upon Ruth was the result of her faithfulness in following the Word of God regarding the law of levirate marriage, which is the law of love.

THE LORD'S ABILITY: A MIRACLE BIRTH

The text clearly states, "And the LORD *enabled* her to conceive, and she gave birth to a son." The word translated "enabled" is the Hebrew word "gave," as in a gift. Obed was God's wedding gift to the couple. Children are always a gift of the Lord (Psalm 127:3).

Ruth displayed an incredible faith. She went through all those years and all of the levirate marriage issues not knowing if she could ever have children. And it turned out that she could not have children except by the Lord's miracle. Miracle births seem to be a normal part of Jewish heritage.

At times a fertile women and potent men are called to childlessness (Matthew 19:12). On the other hand, some infertile women and impotent men are called to be parents. God gives what we need to fulfill His will, not ours. We all have different callings, need different gifts to accomplish the various services that extend His Kingdom and glorify His Name. Producing godliness is always the work of God as the Holy Spirit empowers us.

THE LORD'S LOYALTY: A MIRACLE LIFE

Ruth 4:14-17 — Then the women said to Naomi, "Blessed is the LORD who has not left you without a redeemer today, and may his name become famous in Israel. 15 He will renew your life and sustain you in your old age. For your daughter-in-law, who loves you and who is better to you than seven sons, has given him birth." 16 Then Naomi took the child, laid him in her lap and cared for him. 17 The women living there said, "Naomi has a son."

In this section, Naomi is brought back into the picture. We see God's provision not only to Ruth as a wife and as a mother, but also we see His provision through Ruth as a daughter-in-law to Naomi. God's loyalty is seen through His help in the present (4:14) as well as the hope He gives for the future (4:15-17a).

God's loyalty provides help in the present. The women in Bethlehem were praising the Lord for the impact of the child upon Naomi, "Blessed is the LORD who has not left you without a redeemer today." As Boaz was Ruth's redeemer; so Obed was Naomi's. Boaz redeemed the land for Mahlon, and Obed would inherit and redeem the land for the family. God did not cease from giving a kinsman-redeemer. There would be one in Naomi's old age that would be committed to her welfare. As Naomi lived in the household of Obed, she came to realize that God's grace was her sufficiency.

The women in the community, perhaps, the same women that saw Naomi in her bitterness, now see Naomi in her blessedness. And all the praise went to the Lord, who had not ceased to help her, but provided for her through Ruth's marriage to Boaz and the birth of Obed.

The fact that they said, "May his name become famous in Israel" could be an indication that it was the eighth day and the *Brit Milah* (the covenant of circumcision) for Obed, when the child was publicly named (Ruth 4:16-17). With the redemption of Ruth, the child became a family celebrity with a name that would be impacting Israel. His name would be famous in Israel. This would certainly prove true as the grandfather of King David (Ruth 4:17, 22). A Jewish father and a Moabite mother of faith produced a Jewish Israelite child. Blessed be the Lord! The idea of unequally yoked together is a matter of faith, not ethnicity. (2 Corinthians 6:14-15)[2]

God's loyalty gives hope for the future. The women continued their praise, "May he also be to you a restorer of life" which literally is a "restorer of soul" (*nephesh* in the Hebrew). This is the same idea found in Psalm 23:3: "He restores my soul," where the Lord as our Shepherd brings our soul back to Him.

> 1 Peter 2:25 —For you were continually straying like sheep, but now you have returned to the Shepherd and Guardian of your souls.

Naomi had not only come back to the Land, but she also came back to the Lord. This ministry of God as pictured in the baby redeemer Obed, is a ministry for all God's people to be involved in His redemptive program.

---

2 If that be so, then what about the intermarriage issues in Ezra and Nehemiah? The issue in those sections was the people's involvement in paganism, not their ethnicity that demanded separation of the wives.

James 5:20 —Let him know that he who turns a sinner from the error of his way will save his soul from death, and will cover a multitude of sins.

All of us are to be God's instruments of grace to restore the soul of the lost sheep of the house of Israel, or any other wayward sheep. Obed was a symbol of hope to Naomi, and we each should be a symbol of hope to our brothers, since we are all called to be our brother's keeper by the law of love.

The women continued to encourage Naomi with words, "He will be your *sustainer* of old age." The word translated "sustainer" has primary meaning in the root "to contain as does a vessel." Obed, as a "container," would keep Naomi together. This once more pictures what our God is to all that trust in Him.

Psalm 55:22 —Cast your burden upon the LORD and He will sustain you; He will never allow the righteous to be shaken.

He will never allow the righteous to be shaken. God does not give us merely life-long security, but eternal security. As with Obed, God's sustaining grace is most evident in our family life. We are to care for our aged family as taught in 1 Timothy 5:8. The Lord gave a kinsman, a redeemer, for Naomi's old age that would be committed to her welfare; a life-long security.

1 Timothy 5:8, 16 —But if anyone does not provide for his own, and especially for those of his household, he has denied the faith and is worse than an unbeliever...If any woman who is a believer has widows, she must assist them and the congregation must not be burdened, so that it may assist those who are widows indeed.

Not only are we called to be our brother's keeper, but our parents sustainers as well. Naomi's restoration reveals His loyal faithfulness. God fulfilled and completed her life.

His Loyalty Gave Love In The Past

The women from Bethlehem recognized that hope for the future came from Ruth as they said: "For your daughter-in-law, who loves you and is better to you than seven sons, has given birth to him." They acknowledged Ruth's unfailing love to Naomi as she was the instrument of God's faithful love to her.

We must remember when they first returned from Moab back to Judah, Ruth seemed like "extra baggage" to Naomi; like sticky fly paper that you can't get off your hands. Naomi did not realize the blessing she had from the Lord in Ruth. Now it is obvious to all that God used this Gentile believer to restore the soul of this lost sheep of the house of Israel. God blessed Naomi not only with Ruth, but even more so with raising up a seed to continue the line of Elimelech.

The Torah could not have helped Naomi, but rather hindered, revealing her excursion to Moab as sin. But the loyal love of Ruth was the linchpin to Naomi's restoration. Self-sacrificial love fulfills the law (Romans 13:8-10). Without love there could be no fulfillment of God's decree for us. Faith through love is how we should live.

The women of Bethlehem also recognized that Ruth is the one "who loves you and is better to you than seven sons." Since 'seven' in Hebrew symbolizes completion or perfection, they conveyed an idea that Ruth's love was a perfect love.

Proverbs reminds us, "There is a friend that sticks closer than a brother." And here was a daughter-in-law better than seven sons! The principle is vital to understand: Your value as a person is not determined by your lineage, but by your love; it is not determined by your funds, but by your faithfulness (1 Corinthians 4:2). A person living out Messiah's love is living the greatest life that can be lived. One person's life that lives out the love of Messiah can restore a soul and secure a future. The redemptive life is the greatest life that can be lived on earth by mortal man, for it lives out the very life of the immortal God. By the grace of God, the child was brought through Ruth into the family of Boaz, the love of Naomi and the line of Messiah.

HIS LOYALTY GAVE A LABOR OF LOVE

Ruth 4:16-17a —Then Naomi took the child and laid him in her lap, and became his nurse. 17 The neighbor women gave him a name, saying, "A son has been born to Naomi!" So they named him Obed.

Naomi served as a nanny for Obed. The word for "nurse" in Hebrew (*omenet*) derives from the word faithful. It is understood to be a dry nurse or a nanny. (The word in Hebrew that is normal for wet nurse is *yanaq* from suckle.) For Naomi, this was a return to service for her God in Israel. Her renewed confidence in God was evidenced in sincere service. The Scriptures note, "The neighbor women gave him a name." Perhaps this was common in some situations as in Luke 1:57-63. They called his name saying, "a son has been born to Naomi, and called his name Obed."

It was the care of Naomi to this child, as a mother to a son, which produced the name Obed, which means servant. His name was God-oriented as befitted his calling, and it also reflected upon Naomi's renewed calling. His name was a beautiful reminder of Naomi's service for God in caring for him.

Believers serve those that are called to serve them. Husbands and wives are called to serve each other (Ephesians 5:21-25). Parents are to serve the children that will one day serve them. Leaders are servants to the congregation that equip them to serve (Ephesians 4:12). Yeshua "came to serve and not be served (Matthew 20:28), and we are called to be His servants. Eternal love is seen in selfless service. Selfishness is seen in self-service.

The word "servant" is used for Messiah in Isaiah and Zechariah (Isaiah 41:8-10; 42:18-19; 43:9-10; 44:1-3, 21; 45:4; 48:20, Zechariah 3:8). This glorious suffering Servant is compared to the nation of Israel (Isaiah 42:19; 49:3). The Messiah is also the healing and restoring servant that will restore Israel to God (Isaiah 42:1-7; 49:1-9; 50:4-10; 52:13-53:12). As Ruth's loyal love never gave up on Naomi, so her descendant, Yeshua, wept over Jerusalem, but never forsook His chosen people (Romans 10:31, 11:1).

Ruth represents Gentile believers called to restore the lost sheep of the house of Israel (Ruth 1:16). As Ruth loved Naomi, so Gentile believers are to love the Jewish people and faithfully minister "the mercy they received" (Romans 11:31), providing grace even to embittered souls. Like Ruth's love for Naomi, all Gentile believers are called by God to love and to restore the Jewish people.

For Naomi this restored service in Israel is a basic theme in the Book of Ruth: The Restoration of Naomi, a lost sheep of house of Israel. This can be seen in the following summary outline:

I.   Restoration through Returning, Chapters 1-2

    A.   Returning to the land in grief with Ruth, 1
    B.   Returning to the Lord by grace through Ruth, 2

II. Restoration through Redemption, Chapters 3-4

    A.   Restoration through Ruth's obedience, 3
    B.   Restoration through Ruth's love, 4

The Lord's sovereignty over the fulfillment of redemption, shows the miracle lineage:

Ruth 4:17b-22 —So they named him Obed. He is the father of Jesse, the father of David. Now these are the generations of Perez:

> Perez was the father of Hezron,
> Hezron the father of Ram,
> Ram the father of Amminadab,
> Amminadab the father of Nahshon,
> Nahshon the father of Salmon,
> Salmon the father of Boaz,
> Boaz the father of Obed,
> Obed the father of Jesse,
> and Jesse the father of David.

We now see God's amazing grace at work in Ruth not only as a wife, mother, and daughter-in-law, but also now as matriarch over the line of David.

The Lord had sovereignly secured the kingship by the seed of a godly couple's miracle child. Naomi's restoration, Ruth's redemption-rest and wedding was to produce Obed, so that the line of David would be secured. The line of Messiah was established to bring about the salvation of Jew and Gentile alike (Matthew 1:5). Obed, which means servant would be the father of Jesse. Jesse means my upright one from the Hebrew word *yashah*. Jesse was the father of David which means beloved. The servant that is upright would provide the love of the Father, even the greater son of David, the Messiah Yeshua.

Obed's Relationship To Perez

In His sovereignty, God appointed that the Messiah would come through the seed of Abraham, therefore He has sustained Abraham's descendents down through the ages (Genesis 12:3; 22:18; Galatians 3:14, 16). Furthermore, in order to confirm God's faithfulness, the New Covenant begins, "The record of the genealogy of Yeshua the Messiah, the son of David, the son of Abraham" (Matthew 1:1).

The genealogy demonstrates the sovereignty of God. Tamar by levirate marriage to Judah had twins (Genesis 38:27). Perez' brother's hand came out first from the womb – initially he would have been the firstborn. However his brother's hand went back into the womb and Perez came out ahead of his brother. God sovereignly had the younger Perez as the one through whom the lineage was counted. God was demonstrating that He was sovereignly securing and developing the seed of Abraham and the line of Messiah. There is a parallel between Tamar and Ruth: God used forsaken women and levirate marriage to accomplish His will.

If it was God's sovereign desire to maintain the seed of Abraham, why was Boaz in the line and not Mahlon or Elimelech? God's gracious choice includes the one who lives by faith, and honors the name of God, but excludes those who do not trust in God and thereby dishonor His Name. Elimelech, and then Mahlon, did not realize at the time that their continued disobedience to God would cost them a great deal. In the same way, many people today who are known as believers may not realize the tremendous cost of their disobedience.

Perhaps Mahlon, as taught by his father Elimelech, thought that because they were Israelites it did not matter how they lived. They mistakenly thought that God's promises were attached to their ethnicity, whether they obeyed or not. This describes the sin of presumption. The *Tenach* and New Covenant warn against such arrogance, and it will not go unpunished. For this reason Jewish people were judged in the wilderness after leaving Egypt. Mahlon, like the Hebrews in the wilderness, proved that God will not allow sin to go unchecked and unjudged. On the other hand, Boaz proved that God will always bless the faithful, who trust and follow Him during a famine or harvest. We can learn from Mahlon's mistakes not to be presumptuous about our high calling as children of God in Messiah, "For our God is a consuming fire" (Hebrews 12:29).

Boaz is our encouragement to use our high calling to redeem that which is lost, "For God is not unjust so as to forget your work and the love which you have shown toward His name, in having ministered and in still ministering to the saints" (Hebrews 6:10).

Let us commit ourselves to "love the Lord our God with all our hearts, all our souls and with all of our might" and to seek His honor as we walk by faith in accordance with His Word. The theme of this period and most of the characters in the book of Ruth was: "In those days there was no king in Israel; everyone did what was right in his own eyes" (Judges 21:25). Do not let this verse become the theme of your life.

As you prayerfully walk by faith in accordance with His Word, please consider the faithfulness of Ruth. The life of Ruth serves as an example to all believers showing us how God can use us to reach out to Jewish people with the message of His everlasting love, and loyalty in Messiah.

A genealogy may seem like a strange way to end a book – but the point is this: God is in charge! From Naomi's point of view, she could only see herself as bitter, empty and forsaken by God. Ruth initially seemed useless to Naomi. Nevertheless Ruth became the ordained instrument to bring Naomi back to faith and service, and produce a child to carry on the line. This child would be the link in the great chain from the calling of Abraham to the coming of the king, David, whose greater Son, the Messiah would be the Redeemer of Israel and Savior of the world.

God sovereignly oversees the affairs of His people, and by His grace all their failures and stumbling become redeemed and then more than useful in His great plan. Therefore we may confidently say, "we know God works all things together for good to those that love God, to those called according to His purpose" (Romans 8:28). History is not haphazard. Our lives are not a mistake.

God has a purpose even for all our blunders in His glorious plan that includes Moabites, unfaithful Israelis, and 'over the hill' farmers –and, yes, even us.

Maybe you are presently in 'Moab' and still rebelling against God, come back to the God who loves you – Come to Messiah, who assures us in Matthew 11:28, "Come unto me all that labor and are heavy laden, and I will give you rest." Let His grace complete your life. For as we look at what God promised Abraham, Boaz and you, this is our confidence: what Messiah began in you He will be faithful to complete it!

APPENDIX

IS JEWISH IDENTITY BY PATRILINEAL OR MATRILINEAL DESCENT?

This question has stirred much controversy throughout the history of Israel. The issue of Jewish identity had been developing for a long time and is argued over constantly. Traditional Orthodox Judaism has determined that a child is a Jew only if the mother is Jewish. But is the father's side irrelevant in determining the Jewish identity of a child? Is Jewish identity determined by the ruling of the rabbis, by the pressures of history, or by the teaching of Scripture?

In early biblical history, descent was clearly patrilineal (Exodus 31:2). Abraham was the first Hebrew (Genesis 14:13). Abraham and Sarah would have a son, Isaac, which would establish the line. Isaac and Rebecca would then have a son, Jacob, which would further that line, and Jacob would then have twelve sons, establishing tribal authority. Never once does the idea appear that a daughter would be necessary to maintain the lineage of Israel. After all, both of Joseph's sons, Ephraim and Manasseh, were born of an Egyptian mother, but there is no hint that they were unacceptable as tribal leaders. Simeon's sons were also born of a non-Israeli, and they were considered leaders in Israel as well (Genesis 46:10, Exodus 6:15). Moses' sons were born of a non-Israeli Midianite. The sons of Solomon were of non-Israeli women (1 Kings 10), and so on.

At first, maternal descent was only permitted to determine family inheritance if there were no sons (Numbers 27:1-8). That descent was at issue in such a case shows that the normative view was always patrilineal. In the time of Moses, there was a question as to whether having a Jewish mother (without a Jewish father) was sufficient to make the child an Israeli (Leviticus 24:10-16, 22). In this section the son of an Israeli woman and an Egyptian father is contrasted with the "sons of Israel," clearly showing that the mother's side was not adequate for the child to be considered a son of Israel.

Identity through the father's side seems to have been accepted as normative (Numbers 1:5-15) into the first century AD (Luke 3:23-38) and throughout Biblical history. If matrilineal descent for Jewish identity is not essentially biblical, where does traditional Judaism get its basis for this idea? It comes from an interpretation of Ezra and Nehemiah (*Encyclopedia Judaica*, vol 10, p 54). I believe this is a mistaken interpretation. Ezra and Nehemiah's tenure of leadership was when the remnant of Jewish people returned from Babylon to Israel (Judea). The nation of Israel were no longer a mighty theocracy, but a very small and oppressed minority.

In Ezra, those Jewish men that intermarried with foreign women were ordered to remove their wives and their children (Ezra 9:3). Regarding this matter both Ezra and Nehemiah (Ezra 9:12; Nehemiah 13:25) bring up what was written in Moses:

> Deuteronomy 7:3 —Furthermore, you shall not intermarry with them; you shall not give your daughters to their sons, nor shall you take their daughters for your sons.

But was this pragmatic response (designed to stop the few Jewish returnees from becoming even more diffused by intermarriage with pagans) meant to declare matrilineal descent for Jewish identity? Of course not, for Moses said that intermarriage by either men or women was wrong. The men are noted here, because the Jewish women who had married foreign husbands would be out of the Jewish community, living with their husband's people, and no longer under Ezra's jurisdiction. This harsh decree by Ezra was neither based on matrilineal descent nor meant to establish it. The decree was meant to handle a difficult moral situation, before moral matters worsened. It was meant to stop intermarriage between Jewish followers of *HaShem* and pagans.

No legislation during this time mandated matrilineal descent for Jewish identity. Only after the dispersion of 135 AD did matrilineal descent for Jewish identity became rabbinically normative as recorded in the Talmud (Kiddushin 68b, circa 200-600 AD). The strongest biblical argument is for patrilineal descent. The issue in the Bible regarding the foundation of the faith is "of the Fathers" (Romans 9:5; 11:28), and not "of the Mothers."

Modern traditional Judaism holds a strong difference of opinions. The largest sect of Judaism in America, Reform Judaism, has stated that the father's side counts as much as the mother's side[3]. The most traditional sect, Orthodox Judaism, says that only the mother's side counts.

For example: There is a family where the mother is non-Jewish, but the father is Jewish. Then their children are considered Jewish according to reformed Judaism. To complicate the matter this family are believers in Yeshua as their Messiah. Then Orthodox Judaism would not consider them Jewish for two reasons: the mother is a non-Jew, and because of their faith in Messiah Yeshua. In this case, even if both parents were Jewish, they still would not be considered Jewish because of their faith. The issue is not ethnicity anymore, but also their belief.

In conclusion we have to consider the real question for this matter. First, by what authority will our Jewish identity be defined. Will it be according to the Word of God or the traditions of men? Each of us must decide by what authority we will depend upon for both our faith and our practice.

---

3 http://www.jewishvirtuallibrary.org/jsource/Judaism/patrilineal1.html.

A GLOSSARY OF
JEWISH AND MESSIANIC TERMINOLOGY

BCE – "Before Common Era" also referred to as "BC" (Before Christ).

CE - "Common Era" also referred to as "AD" (Anno Domini), Year of our Lord.

GEZER CALENDAR - The Gezer calendar is a tablet of soft limestone inscribed in a paleo-Hebrew script. It is one of the oldest known examples of Hebrew writing, dating to the 10th century BCE. The calendar describes monthly or bi-monthly periods and attributes to each a duty such as harvest, planting or tending specific crops.

MESSIAH - (Moshiach) Literally, "Anointed One" as a prince, or King of Israel; The Greek equivalent of this Hebrew word is "Christos," which transliterated into English, is "Christ."

OLAM HAZEH - In traditional Judaism "the present age"

OLAM HABA - In traditional Judaism "the world to come."

SEPTUAGINT - "Seventy." Greek translation of the Tenakh by 70 rabbis, appx. 180 BCE.

SHAVUOT - Literally in Hebrew, "weeks."

SHEMA - Literally means hear; The Shema is the prayer from Deuteronomy 6:4.

SUKKOT - Literally Hebrew for booths which means temporary shelter, tabernacle, booth, pavilion, and tents.

SYNAGOGUE - assembly; an adopted Greek word for the House of God—used for prayer, study, and assembly. (see Jacob/James 2:2).

TALMUD - Completed around AD 600, a collection of ancient volumized Jewish commentaries on the Scriptures/ Torah. The Talmud is made up of the older rabbinical comments called Mishnah, and later rabbinical comments on the Mishnah known as Gemara. Traditional Judaism holds to these as authoritative, equal to, even superior to the Scriptures.

TENAKH - The Hebrew Scriptures, or "Old Testament." Tenakh is an acronym made up of three Hebrew letters: TORAH (The Five Books of Moses); NEVIIM (The Prophets); KETUVIM (The Writings: Job, Psalms, Prov., Eccles., Song of Solomon)

TORAH - Literally means "Instruction." Also, known as the first five books of Moses.

YESHUA - In Hebrew literally means salvation. Yeshua is the equivalent to the English word Jesus. See Matthew 1:21.

YOM KIPPUR -literally in Hebrew *yom*- "day"; *kippur*- "covering"/ "atonement".

TARGUM -A "Targum" is a translation, but the term is usually used specifically to designate Aramaic translations of the Bible. According to an ancient Jewish tradition, the public reading of the Bible in the synagogue must be accompanied by a translation into Aramaic, which was the spoken language of most Jews in Israel and Babylonia during the Talmudic era.

ADDENDUM

These studies on the book of Ruth have come from many years of my personal study and teaching this wonderful book. The works listed below had an influence on my study of Ruth, and I trust they will bless you in your further studies as well.

Barber, Cyril J., *Ruth: An Expositional Commentary*, Moody Press, 1983

Cox and Fuller, *The Book of Ruth*, Klock & Klock Christian Publishers Inc, 1982

Cox, Samuel, *The Book of Ruth: A Devotional Commentary*, The Religious Tract Society

Cundall and Morris, *Judges & Ruth*, Inter-Varsity Press, 1968

Dallas Seminary Faculty, *The Bible Knowledge Commentary: An Exposition of the Scripture*, SP Publications, 1985

Dehaan, M R, *The Romance of Redemption*, Zondervan Publishing House, 1958

Gardiner, George E, *The Romance of Ruth*, Kregel Publications, 1977

Goslinga, C J, *Joshua, Judges, Ruth*, Zondervan Publishing House, 1986

Henry, Matthew, *Matthew Henry's Commentary Vol. 1: Genesis to Deuteronomy*, MacDonald Publishing Company

Heslop, William G, *Rubies from Ruth*, Kregel Publications, 1944

Hession, Roy, *Our Nearest Kinsman*, Christian Literature Crusade, 1976

Jamieson, Robert, *A Commentary: Critical, Experimental, and practical Vol. 1*, William B. Eerdmans Publishing Company, 1982

Keil and Delitzsch, *Commentary on the Old Testament Vol. 2: Joshua, Judges, Ruth, 1 & 2 Samuel*, William B. Eerdmans Publishing Company, 1976

Lange, John Peter, *Lange's Commentary on the Scriptures Vol.2: Numbers-Ruth*, Zondervan Publishing House, 1960

McGee, J Vernon, *Ruth: The Romance of Redemption*, Van Kampen Press 1954

Morison, James, *The Pulpit Commentary Vol. 4: Ruth 1 & 2 Samuel*, William B. Eerdmans Publishing Company, 1950

Scherman, Nosson, *Megillas Ruth*, Mesorah Publications Ltd, 1976

To these and many others, I am truly indebted and thankful.

Books and Materials by
Word of Messiah Ministries

Messianic Life Lessons from the Book of Jonah -the book of Jonah reveals a Holy, Almighty God who loves people desperately, and will go to any lengths, or depths to reach lost and sinful people. In this book you will discover God's purpose and plan for Jonah's life and learn from Jonah not to flee His will, but rather follow God's will.

Messiah in the Feasts of Israel - God's redemptive plan is unveiled through the feasts of Israel. Discover how God's appointed times are still relevant for our lives today and how they point to our glorious future with Messiah.

The Messianic Answer Book - Jewish Answers to Jewish Questions about the Jewish Messiah. This book answers to the 14 most common questions Jewish people have about the Jewish Messiah. An excellent tool to share with those seeking answers.

Following Yeshua: Foundational Discipleship for Messianic Believers - Develop a solid foundation by learning the basic truths needed to grow in God's love.

Growing in Messiah: Vital Truths for Maturing Messianic Believers - Answers to challenging questions faced by Jewish and non-Jewish believers in Yeshua. Can be used as a sequel to "Following Yeshua."

Messianic Wisdom: Practical Scriptural Answers for Your Life - Discover your Jewish roots, get a better grasp on Jewish issues and living out your faith in Messiah. Essential, practical, and inspiring, this book is a must for every growing disciple of Yeshua.

SENSE & SENSIBILITY: Honoring God with my life -In this expositional study of Titus 2:3-5, you will discover how to live a life of true satisfaction and reward. This book will not only help you to grow and mature in the qualities from Titus 2:3-5, but also will equip you to mentor and disciple other women.

EVEN YOU CAN SHARE THE JEWISH MESSIAH! - Share your faith with Jewish people in a sensitive, effective manner. "Do's and Don'ts", history of 'the Church' and the Jews, prophecy chart.

THE MESSIANIC PASSOVER HAGGADAH - The perfect guide for conducting your own Passover Seder, for family or congregational use, or to simply learn more about Messiah and Passover.

IS JESUS THE MESSIAH? A Study of Isaiah 53 - A four message series with an in-depth look at the Scriptures, history, and ancient rabbinical comments, that proves conclusively that Yeshua truly is the Jewish Messiah (CDs or Audio cassette).

TO THE JEW 1ST! - God's priority of taking the Gospel to the Jewish community from Romans 1:16,17; how to share with Jewish friends from The Jewish Evangelism Seminar. (9 Msgs., CDs / Tapes)

HOLOCAUST: A Biblical Response - A two tape, four message series including *Yom HaShoah/*Holocaust Remembrance Service, testimony of Holocaust survivor, *Anti-Semitism is Anti-God*, and *Escape Israel's Future Holocaust* (Zech. 14). Moving, informative, and challenging. (4 msgs., CDs / Tapes)

For more information, please contact us at:

WORD OF MESSIAH MINISTRIES
P.O. BOX 79238
CHARLOTTE, NC
28271, USA

PHONE/FAX: (704) 362-1927

Visit our website at:

WWW.WORDOFMESSIAH.ORG

"Messianic Life Lessons from the book of Ruth"
by Sam Nadler
Copyright © 2006 by Sam Nadler
Word of Messiah Ministries
All rights reserved.
Printed in the United States of America

ISBN-13: 978-0-9786568-0-5